Making Successful Decisions in Counselling and Psychotherapy

A Practical Guide

Making Successful Decisions in Counselling and Psychotherapy

A Practical Guide

David A. Lane and Sarah Corrie

Mc Graw Hill   Open University Press

Open University Press
McGraw-Hill Education
McGraw-Hill House
Shoppenhangers Road
Maidenhead
Berkshire
England
SL6 2QL

email: enquiries@openup.co.uk
world wide web: www.openup.co.uk

and Two Penn Plaza, New York, NY 10121-2289, USA

First published 2012

A catalogue record of this book is available from the British Library

ISBN-13: 9780335244348
ISBN-10: 0335244343
e-ISBN: 9780335244355

Library of Congress Cataloging-in-Publication Data
CIP data has been applied for

Typeset by Aptara Inc., India
Printed in the UK by Bell and Bain Ltd, Glasgow.

Fictitious names of companies, products, people, characters and/or data that may be used herein (in case studies or in examples) are not intended to represent any real individual, company, product or event.

MIX
Paper from
responsible sources
FSC
www.fsc.org   FSC® C007785

The McGraw·Hill Companies

Praise for this book

"It is commonly assumed that the ability to make decisions in therapy is acquired as a result of experience and for this reason the subject is more or less ignored in programmes of training. Lane and Corrie effectively challenge this position in a comprehensive account of the process by which information is acquired, interpreted and used. The book benefits from the comprehensive experience of the two authors both as clinicians and researchers and is illustrated by some excellent case material and interesting self-assessment exercises. There is something of value here for therapists of every modality at all stages of development."
—Ray Woolfe, Psychologist and Psychotherapist in independent practice (Bristol), UK

"In this well written, meticulously researched and timely book, Lane and Corrie propose that the art of decision making, like any art, requires discipline, training and continual practice. This book should be required reading on clinical and counselling psychology programmes and related fields. For those about to enter practice, this book provides you with much needed support for engaging with the realities of a complex and shifting political and professional landscape. For the more experienced practitioner, this book challenges you to become more explicit about, and to sharpen and widen, the assumptions, models and procedures that guide your everyday decision making. This is continuing professional development of the most relevant and needed kind. I will be recommending this text to my students, colleagues, peers, and, yes, managers, very strongly indeed!"
—Dr Michael Worrell, Consultant Clinical Psychologist, CNWL Foundation NHS Trust & Royal Holloway University of London, UK

"In this book Lane and Corrie have made an important contribution to the training of counsellors and therapists, and the practice of working in the helping professions – and they have managed to do this in a way that is engaging, accessible and practical. Whether you are just starting out in the helping professions, or are a seasoned therapist, this book will help you improve your practice. The case studies, illustrations and reflection questions bring to life the dynamics of decision making and provide the reader with useful pathways to more sophisticated and effective decision making in their work."

—Dr Michael Cavanagh, Coaching Psychology Unit, Sydney University, Australia and Visiting Professor, Institute of Work Based Learning, Middlesex University, UK

"Lane and Corrie draw upon their rich experience and understanding not just as clinicians and researchers but also as adult educators to provide a book which deepens our understanding of decision making. The insights and approach put forward go beyond the professional context which illustrates them to contribute to a broader understanding of what it is or what it might be to be a professional and to take professional decisions in an increasingly complex and rapidly changing world. When considering how good decision makers develop the key insight is to focus our attention upon the learning process rather than knowledge content. This change of viewpoint is profound."

—Professor Jonathan Garnett, Director Institute for Work Based Learning, Middlesex University, UK

Contents

List of exercises   ix
Foreword   xi
Acknowledgements   xiii
The authors   xv
Introduction   1

Part I: What do we know about decision-making in counselling and psychotherapy?

1 Decision-making under the microscope   11

2 Beyond the question of accuracy: decision-making in
   the real world   31

3 Going wider, going deeper: decision-making in states
   of uncertainty   47

Part II: How do we frame our decision-making in practice?

4 MAP: a framework for decision-making in practice   65

5 Defining your Mission   71

6 Identifying the Attitude that informs your decisions   87

7 Devising a Process for decision-making   107

Part III: Decision-making contexts that require special consideration

8 Decision-making in supervision   131

9 Decision-making in teams   151

10 Developing as a critical thinker: some final recommendations   165

References   175
Index   187

List of exercises

Exercise 1. What do you know about your decision-making skills?   7
Exercise 2. Working with Emily's low self-esteem. What would
             you do?   13
Exercise 3. Which biases tend to operate in your thinking?   19
Exercise 4. What kind of causal analyst are you?   21
Exercise 5. Correcting a heuristic error. What would you do?   22
Exercise 6. What are your therapy schemas?   24
Exercise 7. Analysing a decision that proved to be unhelpful   28
Exercise 8. What foundational beliefs underpin therapy?   32
Exercise 9. Working with fairy or folk tales as an example of the
             implicational domain   41
Exercise 10. Which thinking skills do you use?   43
Exercise 11. Seeking to understand clients' expectations when they
             meet you   48
Exercise 12. Using the six thinking hats to take a different perspective   54
Exercise 13. Using Chapman's integration to take a wider perspective   56
Exercise 14. Working with presence   58
Exercise 15. Approaching tensions in complex spaces   60
Exercise 16. How do you seek to define your Mission?   77
Exercise 17. Establishing the super objective for your role as therapist   79
Exercise 18. Identifying the factors that have shaped your Perspective   91
Exercise 19. Which field of vision is dominant for you?   103
Exercise 20. Auditing your range of decision-making tools   109
Exercise 21. Pulling it all together   127
Exercise 22. Auditing your experiences of supervision   132
Exercise 23. Towards developing a shared supervisory Mission   139
Exercise 24. Clarifying the Attitude at work in your supervision   143
Exercise 25. Decision-making in the supervision process   145
Exercise 26. What is your experience of teams?   152
Exercise 27. Therapist dilemma. What would you do?   156
Exercise 28. Putting it to the test: does Kayes's theory fit your
             experience?   160
Exercise 29. Planning your future performance as a team member   163

Foreword

Counsellors and psychotherapists often tend to fall into one of two categories situated at opposite ends of the decision-making continuum. At one end there exists a large grouping who when it comes to decision making tend to fall back upon an intuitive 'this is how it's done' perspective. They base choices upon personal experience without much detailed thought to the reasoning behind the decisions they make. At the other extreme are those therapists who adopt a somewhat formulaic or standardized approach to decision making. For them the decision-making process is followed rather rigidly in a step-by-step manner, without too much attention paid to its appropriateness to the particular client case in question – ie. the crucial aspect of context.

David Lane and Sarah Corrie challenge the assumption that the skills inherent in decision making are acquired automatically through experience. Knowing what works and what doesn't work is as relevant to therapy as to any other field of activity, yet as the authors point out, it is neglected in formal professional training. The result of this is that too often training programmes focus on acquiring learning through content which is discipline-specific as opposed to understanding the learning process, a sometimes more involved method which involves an emphasis on how to acquire, interpret and use information.

Much of the literature on decision making is concerned with accuracy, with getting it right. However, it can be argued that this overlooks the richness and complexity of working therapeutically with clients. At any point, multiple decisions may have to be made and there may be more than one course of action that could be facilitative for the client. Many decisions in therapy are therefore made in states of uncertainty.

As David and Sarah explain, therapists must 'embrace ambiguity' and the individual therapist's ability to cope with this is an important factor. They suggest that to manage complex and non-linear decision-making scenarios, it is helpful to think about practice as taking place in a number of different professional spaces. They describe these as rational, emergent and chaotic, depending respectively upon 1) whether there is a high level of agreement about what to do; 2) having only a moderate likelihood of determining outcomes; or finally 3) a situation in which there is little or no agreement about what to do and in which outcomes cannot be predicted with any accuracy.

Having introduced the reader to the skills and styles of reasoning involved in decision making, David and Sarah seek to identify some of the capabilities and styles of reasoning necessary for good decision making. In doing so they offer a framework they call MAP, an acronym for Mission, Attitude and Process, which can be used with clients at each stage of the therapeutic process. They see this framework as offering the potential to address a range of professional practice dilemmas.

The strength of this book is rooted in the considerable experience of the two authors both as clinicians and researchers. It is soundly based on psychological theory and research and on clinical practice, and there is a variety of case material bringing together theory and practice. The experience of the authors as trainers is also apparent in the direct manner in which the reader is addressed and encouraged to reflect upon self through the inclusion of self-assessment exercises throughout.

Ray Woolfe

Acknowledgements

There are a number of people who have contributed to the development of this book and whose interest and support we would like to acknowledge.

We thank Monika Lee, our editor, and everyone at Open University Press who has helped bring this project to completion.

We are grateful to all those who, over the years, have shaped our understanding of decision-making. Many clients who cannot be named have influenced our thinking – our thanks to them. To our colleagues at the Professional Development Foundation (PDF) in various programmes worldwide who have experimented with and critiqued the emerging ideas, our heartfelt thanks.

David Lane wishes to acknowledge Mary Bruce who first introduced him to careful listening to client stories. Also Vic Meyer, Ted Chesser, Michael Bruch and Mary Watts at Middlesex Hospital and University College London, and the team at Islington Educational Guidance Centre, especially Fiona Green, Julius Malkin, Peggy Gosling and Robin Miller. Additionally, thanks are due to Edward de Bono who encouraged his interest in thinking skills, and to Ray Woolfe and colleagues on British Psychological Society (BPS) committees in counselling psychology, Sheelagh Strawbridge and colleagues on the BPS Psychotherapy Register, and colleagues in the British Association for Counselling & Psychotherapy, the European Association for Counselling and the European Federation of Psychologists' Associations Psychotherapy Committee with whom he has shared his professional journey.

Sarah Corrie would also like to thank her colleagues and students on the Postgraduate Diploma and MSc in Cognitive Behavioural Psychotherapy at Central and North West London NHS Foundation Trust. Their talent and skills, successes and dilemmas have provided the inspiration for many of the ideas presented in this book.

We are particularly grateful to both Lloyd Chapman and Nancy Kline for permission to draw upon their work.

Finally, special thanks go to Diana Osborne for critique and support. Special thanks also go to Ian Lacey for his encouragement and critique, proof-reading duties, and for devoting time and energy to the realization of this project in many different ways.

Case material

Unless stated otherwise, the case studies used in this book are genuine and derived from work that the authors have conducted over many years of professional practice. They have, however, been adapted to meet the needs of this book. In order to protect confidentiality, names and details have been changed and certain case examples represent an amalgam of several individuals or work-based scenarios.

The authors

David Lane is a chartered psychologist and director of the Professional Development Foundation. He contributes to leading-edge research in coaching as well as supervising leading coaches undertaking doctoral research. He was chair of the British Psychological Society (BPS) Register of Psychologists Specialising in Psychotherapy and convenor of the Psychotherapy Group of the European Federation of Psychologists' Associations. His work with the European Mentoring and Coaching Council has been concerned with codes of conduct and standards, and kite marking of coach training. Working with the Worldwide Association of Business Coaches, he has researched and developed the standards for the Certified Master Business Coach award. He is a founder of the Global Convention on Coaching.

He was an honorary senior lecturer at University College Medical School, honorary senior research fellow at City University and visiting professor at Syracuse University as well as currently at Middlesex University. He is a recipient of the Senior Award of the Counselling Psychology Division (BPS) for 'outstanding scientific contribution' which follows both Fellowship of the BPS and an earlier national Freedom of Information award for his work on sharing client information. In 2010 he received the BPS award for Distinguished Contribution to Professional Psychology.

Sarah Corrie is a consultant clinical psychologist and chartered psychologist. She received her undergraduate degree in psychology and counselling psychology from the University of Surrey. Recipient of the Professors Newstead and Gale Prize in recognition of 'an exceptionally high standard of attainment in examination and course work', she then went on to obtain her doctorate in clinical psychology at Canterbury Christchurch College before completing her post-doctoral training in cognitive behaviour therapy at the University of Oxford.

Sarah has extensive experience in both public and private sector services and runs her own practice, as well as working as a freelance writer, trainer and lecturer. She is programme director of the postgraduate diploma and MSc in cognitive behavioural psychotherapy offered by Central and North West London NHS Foundation Trust in conjunction with Royal Holloway, University of London. She has extensive experience in supervising, training and lecturing practitioners in the fields of psychology, psychiatry and counselling. Sarah is also a member of faculty of the Professional Development Foundation.

Sarah has a background in the performing arts and has maintained involvement through her membership with Equity and the Imperial Society of Teachers of Dancing.

Introduction

The task of working with a client in order to bring about therapeutic change involves a constant stream of decisions, choices and judgements. But how exactly do you make these decisions? What influences your choices and how can you be sure that you are making the 'right' ones for a particular client, at a particular point in time?

Training provides guidelines, as do the services and professional bodies that govern our practice once we are qualified. However, even these cannot provide definitive instruction.

Therapeutic decision-making is a challenging business. This complexity is compounded by the social, economic and political climate in which therapists work. The demands of the work place are becoming increasingly complex, with the funding of many services highly uncertain. The rapid pace of change makes it difficult to predict what type of knowledge will be required in the future (Stice 1987). Becher and Chassin (2001: 74) even go as far as asserting that 'the only surety is that today's knowledge is obsolete tomorrow'.

Arguably, more is being demanded of today's professionals than ever before. What can be predicted is that all those involved in addressing human concerns will need to be equipped with tools for decision-making that remain relevant and useful as the available knowledge-base evolves.

The case for becoming a successful decision-maker

This book is about helping you become a successful thinker and decision-maker. Regardless of the service in which you are seeing clients or your preferred way of working, the need to make choices is unavoidable. The decisions you face will include whether or not to work with a client, deciding on the main focus of your work together and developing intervention plans that are fit for purpose. They will also include making choices about any general and discipline-specific knowledge you need in order to work effectively and how best you can develop your decision-making potential over the course of your career.

Educators in most, if not all, disciplines believe that it is vital to equip their students with the requisite thinking skills that enable them to perform effectively in the work place. Nonetheless, in our experience it is relatively rare for professional therapy training to provide explicit instruction on skills in decision-making. We believe that many practitioners (experienced therapists, as well as those starting out in their careers) may be at a disadvantage through not having had access to formal training in the specific mental operations of decision-making.

Why might a skill that is so highly valued in principle be neglected in formal professional training? We believe that this can be linked to an assumption that these skills are acquired automatically through experience. As a result, professional training focuses on acquiring learning about content (i.e. discipline-specific knowledge) rather than process (the methods used for acquiring, interpreting and using this information). For example, during their training, students are expected to observe and emulate role models who have considerable expertise in both discipline-specific knowledge and reasoning abilities. However, experts do not necessarily have a good understanding of their own reasoning skills (Kassirer et al. 1982); expertise is internalized over time and therefore not readily accessible to articulation or, therefore, teaching to others (Ericsson and Smith 1991). Moreover, for reasons that we shall explore, the literature that exists is not always entirely suited to the decision-making task in hand and there remains a paucity of guidance on how to develop context-sensitive decision-making skills.

Decision-making in the 'real world' is difficult and professional practice makes many cognitive demands of those who provide counselling and psychotherapy services. In our culture there is sometimes a tendency to overlook this and to reach for simplistic formulae that promise simple 'step-by-step' solutions. In a society that favours clearly defined problems, operationalized goals, and measurable results, it is not surprising that many of us feel a certain aversion towards complexity and ambiguity.

Simplistic formulae can be extremely useful when the problems themselves are relatively straightforward. But they can also convey a degree of simplicity that does not exist in the real world and, if interpreted as offering uncomplicated solutions to complex endeavours, can ultimately mislead more than they enlighten. As O'Donohue et al. (1990) observe, there remains a lack of consensus about what constitutes optimal clinical decision-making or indeed what defines a 'good decision'. For this reason, we have avoided any simple templates or checklists that promise a 'how to do it' approach. We do not promise a 'recipe' for success (to the best of our knowledge there is no verified formula across all contexts). Rather, we aim to identify some of the capabilities necessary for good decision-making and provide a set of maxims for the tasks with which therapy confronts us. This, in turn, is underpinned by the assumption that decision-making is a discipline in its own right.

What this book is about

This book is about helping you become a successful thinker and decision-maker in your professional life as a counsellor, psychologist or psychotherapist.[1] It will help you develop a robust approach through combining knowledge derived from the current literature with tools and exercises to aid skill development. It also offers a practical guide that can help you navigate the choices that are typical of everyday therapy practice. More specifically, you will:

- learn about the literature on clinical judgement and professional decision-making so that you are aware of some of the challenges of making successful decisions;
- complete exercises to hone your decision-making skills;
- discover a framework for making effective choices that you can apply to your work, regardless of context and setting;
- explore the issues that are faced by trying to innovate outside of existing guidelines and learn some principles for approaching such innovations in a systematic way.

By learning about these areas you will be able to:

- improve how you think (not just what you think);
- develop specific skills in therapeutic decision-making that can assist you in different aspects of your practice;
- identify those factors that are shaping your professional judgement, so you can capitalize on helpful sources of influence and minimize unhelpful ones;
- make your decision-making more transparent (to yourself and others, including your clients) and thus more open to critique and refinement.

In order to achieve these aims we draw on a range of resources including the current literature on clinical decision-making, models drawn from education and leadership, ideas from different therapeutic schools, case vignettes and problem-solving exercises. We will also draw on our own experience as decision-makers. As experienced practitioners, supervisors and trainers, we face challenges in how to make successful decisions every day. But we have also learned some valuable lessons along the way and will be sharing these with you as you go about developing your own skills. This 'sharing' will sometimes take the form of specific recommendations and advice, and at other times anecdotes and stories which we hope will be both entertaining and thought-provoking.

You will find that each chapter includes exercises which are designed to help you consider the implications of the ideas for your own practice. We would warmly encourage you to engage with these exercises as they will help you gain more from the book.

An overview of the book

This book consists of three parts.

In Part 1 we introduce you to the literature on decision-making to give you a good grounding in the debates that have characterized the field to date. *Chapter 1* examines the debate on the accuracy of therapists' decision-making and gives you some tools for improving the accuracy of your clinical judgement. *Chapter 2* takes a more critical view of the literature and proposes that while accuracy is vital to effective therapeutic thinking, it is not the whole story. This paves the way for identifying other reasoning skills that are needed to offer an optimum service to clients. In *Chapter 3* we examine the range of reasoning skills that therapists need in order to work effectively with clients, and that have been neglected in the literature to date – most notably, thinking skills in innovation and design. We offer methods for helping you develop these skills in your own practice.

Having identified and evaluated some of the key debates and skills that are needed, we move on to Part 2 of the book. In *Chapter 4*, we introduce you to the MAP framework by providing a brief, general overview. MAP (an acronym for 'Mission–Attitude–Process') is a framework that has been shown to be effective across a range of professional practice settings. In *Chapters 5–7* we use this framework to consider, in detail, the different types of decisions and choices that are particularly relevant at each stage of therapeutic work.

Part 3 looks at the application of MAP and the decision-making principles covered in the previous parts of the book to two specific contexts in which decision-making skills are vital: supervision and team working. In Part 3 we also conclude the book by drawing together, in *Chapter 10*, the material from the previous parts to provide some general conclusions about how therapists make choices. We offer what we call a 'reflective tool' which enables you to synthesize your key points of learning along the way. This tool represents one means through which you can reflect upon, critique and refine your work and which we offer as an aid to reflective practice, discussion in supervision and as a means of supporting your career development.

Intended audience

This book is intended to appeal to a wide audience. Because decision-making is vital to all therapies, it will complement core texts in any and all therapeutic modalities. It has relevance to all those involved in providing psychological, psychotherapeutic and counselling interventions and is accessible to practitioners at all stages of their careers, including those undergoing their first core professional training. More experienced practitioners, who seek a conceptual and practical guide that can assist them in critiquing and refining their work, will also find this a valuable resource. The book will also be of benefit to trainers and supervisors looking for an effective means of assisting their students in developing decision-making skills.

How to use this book

This book encourages you to examine how you respond to the many dilemmas you encounter in therapy practice, and to produce a map of the factors that do and should feature in your decision-making. It aims to help you compile a personal portfolio of knowledge, evidence, processes and techniques that will support you in your work. As such, this is designed to be an interactive text. Our task is to help you navigate the different ideas and approaches presented. Your task is to transform everything you read into a form that makes sense for you.

It is also important to be aware that the literature on decision-making and problem-solving is vast, rapidly expanding and, in places, extremely complex. Although we have structured this book in a way that makes the ideas as accessible and practical as possible, we would be misrepresenting both the decision sciences and professional practice if we attempted to over-simplify the theories and models which are emerging. For these reasons some sections of this book are, of necessity, more complex than others.

So before you get under way we would like to encourage you to think about your current stage of career development and what it is you most need from reading this book. To practise a discipline is to be a lifelong learner, and part of the skill in planning and organizing your professional development is knowing where to 'pitch' your efforts at any point in time. You want to select those exercises and ideas that make most sense to you, at this stage in your career, for the context in which you are working. In the same way that experienced therapists know when to work with a client and when to refer them elsewhere, it is important that you can decide which ideas you will work with and which ones (for now) you will pass over.

If, for example, you are at the start of your career and perhaps undergoing your core professional training as a counsellor or psychotherapist, you may find yourself feeling anxious about how much you have to learn and wonder what specific steps you can take to improve the quality of your thinking in a general way. If this is true for you, then you may wish to restrict your reading to Part 1 of this book to begin with, to familiarize yourself with some of the key debates, work on improving the accuracy of your professional judgement and learn some tips for developing a more robust and systematic approach.

If you are a more experienced decision-maker, find yourself working with clients in complex circumstances or are providing services in organizations undergoing major reconfiguration, you will find Parts 2 and 3 particularly helpful. Professional practice can take place in many different 'spaces', each of which requires a different decision-making response. When we move into more complex decision-making scenarios, the problems themselves are very difficult to define and give rise to high levels of uncertainty or anxiety. Therapists will need the ability to assess whether they are psychologically and technically prepared for this type of work, the adequacy of the supervisory and support structures available to enable it, and an ability to know when it becomes unsafe to work with a client in that particular service setting. If you are not at a stage in your career where you need to engage in these more complex decision-making scenarios, you might wish to skim over these parts of the book and return to them when your professional development needs require you to do so.

Do also give some thought to what you might need to support you through the process. We would recommend that you take time to build a relationship with the ideas presented and to explore how they relate to your practice. We highly recommend that you invest in a journal or notebook that can become a personal learning log. Your learning log is the place for recording any insights, realizations, thoughts or questions that occur to you as you go along. An electronic journal might also be useful to help you search and link ideas.

It is important to be aware that the ideas discussed in this book are not a substitute for appropriately supervised practice. They are designed to aid your learning and development but not to replace formal training. Indeed, you may need access to adequate support when it comes to experimenting with some of the concepts discussed in this book, particularly some of the complex ideas. We would also like to encourage you to discuss them with colleagues, supervisors and trainers (and if you are a supervisor or trainer yourself, your students). In fact, taking them to supervision and discussing them with your colleagues is something that we would highly recommend.

And finally...

The aim of this book is to help you become better at thinking. It is an invitation to step back from your usual decision-making style, and your usual thinking habits, so that you can critique and refine your existing approach and explore some new ways of approaching the dilemmas to which therapy practice often gives rise.

While we cannot, or perhaps should not, ever be sure we have 'perfected' decision-making in therapy, we can hone our skills in this area. Indeed, there is some evidence that decision-making and problem-solving skills can be reliably improved by systematic training (see Greenfield 1987), and a general finding in the literature (for a review, see Cotton 1991) is that thinking skills programmes make a positive difference in the achievement levels of those who participate. Of course, any discipline takes time, effort and practice to master. However, reading this book is a good start. If you are hoping to become a skilled thinker (and we hope that this is what you aspire to) be prepared to work hard. Ultimately, the effort will be worth it!

To begin the journey, we invite you to complete the following exercise:

Exercise 1: *What do you know about your decision-making skills?*

The aim of this exercise is to help you think about your own approach to decision-making.

A. Identify a time when you made a good decision. This can be a decision you made in your therapy practice, or it may be decision you made in another area of your life.

- What was the situation?
- How did you know it was a 'good' decision?
- What were the resources you drew upon that enabled you to make this decision?
- What influenced your decision in this case (for good or ill)?

B. Now identify a time when you made what you would judge to be a poor decision.

- What was the situation?
- How did you know it was a 'poor' decision?
- What were the resources you drew upon that led you to make this decision?
- What influenced your decision in this case (for good or ill)?

Looking across both examples, what can you conclude about your approach to decision-making? What were the factors operating in each case? Can you identify any processes or criteria that helped shape the result you obtained? Write any insights you may have had in your learning log.

Reference

1. For the purposes of this book, the titles of counsellor, therapist and practitioner are used interchangeably as the content relates to all of those who are offering therapy services to clients.

Part I

What do we know about decision-making in counselling and psychotherapy?

In Part 1 (Chapters 1–3) of this book, you will become familiar with the reasoning skills involved in successful decision-making. We examine the literature on decision-making. We consider the strengths and limitations of this literature in helping us develop a better understanding of how therapists think, make decisions, and implement their decisions in real-world therapy contexts. We also identify some of the principal thinking skills and approaches to reasoning that practitioners need if they are to operate as effective therapists, including analysis, critical thinking, creativity, innovation and design, and how the acquisition of these different mental operations may need to be achieved through different types of learning.

1 Decision-making under the microscope

In this chapter you will learn about:

- the literature on decision-making
- the implications of this literature for therapy practice
- methods to assess and improve the accuracy of your judgements

By reading this chapter you will be able to:

- assess your own decision-making approach
- analyse the accuracy your decisions
- overcome common biases in decision-making
- identify key questions you need to consider to build a decision-making model

Introduction

As professional practitioners, we take pride in our skills in judgement and reasoning. In applying ourselves to the puzzles we encounter in our work, we claim to facilitate insights and offer solutions that are different from those that our clients can arrive at by themselves. Arguably, this is what justifies our claims to professional status. But how exactly do we make these judgements?

What separates us from the public we seek to serve is our familiarity with the theory, models and evidence base of counselling and psychotherapy and our ability to apply this knowledge in systematic and effective ways. This implies an approach to decision-making that is rational and logical. However, we must consider whether or not these claims are justified in light of the research literature that has investigated the quality, and in particular the accuracy, of decision-making in professional practice.

In this chapter we introduce you briefly to the literature on clinical judgement and decision-making and use this as a basis for helping you assess your own decision-making approach. We present frameworks that can help you identify specific decision-making 'traps' and offer methods for systematically improving the quality of the judgements you make.

As you familiarize yourself with the different ideas presented and work through each of the exercises, we recommend that you write notes in your learning log for discussion in supervision, in tutorials or with colleagues. This will help you personalize the debates to your own learning needs.

To begin this process, we would like to engage you in an exercise which illustrates a decision that therapists have to make in all types of therapy, with all types of clients – namely, how to make sense of a client's request for help.

Case study: How to help Emily with her low self-esteem

Imagine that you are meeting a new client, Emily, who is requesting help with overcoming low self-esteem. As Emily's therapist, you need to establish what her needs are, what would be the best way to proceed and whether you are in a position to provide this service. As a result, you decide that if you are to help her find a useful way forward, you must gain a better understanding of what Emily means by 'low self-esteem'.

At this point, a number of possibilities present themselves. Depending on how Emily tells her story, and the nature of the difficulties she describes, it may emerge that she is experiencing low self-esteem in the context of depression. Prior to becoming depressed she had had a healthy self-regard. Based on this understanding, you begin to hypothesize that if she receives treatment for her depression, her low self-esteem should resolve by itself. Your decision – grounded in this initial hypothesis – may be to share your hunch with Emily and provide information on the common symptoms of depression to see if these 'fit' with her experience. You might also use a range of questionnaires to establish the validity of your hunch. Should this be supported, and the client is in agreement, you may decide to organize therapy around treating depression.

Alternatively, Emily's low self-esteem may be a consequence of a change in her health status. Her medical condition has implications for her lifestyle and career, and her former view of herself as strong and capable has been undermined as a result. In this case, you begin to consider an intervention plan that focuses on helping her come to terms with the deterioration in her health, developing effective problem-solving skills for managing difficult situations and enhancing her repertoire of coping skills. You might also consider drawing on the services of other agencies, such as support groups and benefit or employment agencies, to ensure that Emily's needs are adequately met. If Emily believes that this course of action is likely to result in an improved quality of life, you have a basis for moving forward in your work together.

Then again, you may begin to suspect that her low self-esteem is an enduring vulnerability factor. When she refers to 'low self-esteem', Emily is in fact describing a long-standing, highly troubled relationship with herself that is associated with extreme levels of self-loathing and self-condemnation and which you suspect is indicative of a deeper level of personality disturbance. As Emily tells you her story, it may be that you uncover recurrent self-harming behaviour and patterns of significant difficulty with emotional regulation that lead you to wonder whether a referral to a specialist service for personality disorders would be appropriate.

These are just three of many different possibilities that might arise from exploring what Emily means when she complains of 'low self-esteem'. Each decision will depend on the questions that you ask, your knowledge and experience of working with self-esteem and other client difficulties, and your choices in response to each stage of her unfolding story.

Exercise 2: *Working with Emily's low self-esteem. What would you do?*

If Emily were your client, how would you approach the task of finding out more about her low self-esteem as a basis for planning a way forward? Use the questions below to guide you and write your answers in your learning log.

- What specific questions would you ask the client in order to learn more about her low self-esteem?
  - Why would you ask these questions – how do you think they would help you?
- What questions would you not ask the client?
  - Why do you consider that questions such as these would be unnecessary or unhelpful?

- What methods other than interviewing might you use, if any, to inform your decision-making?
  - This might include self-report questionnaires, interviewing a relative, asking the client to keep records of challenging incidents, or drawing on a colleague's or supervisor's experience in this area.
- What other factors might inform your choice?
  - This might include the literature on low self-esteem, your preferred therapeutic approach, your supervisor's view, the client's preference and the way your service is set up, among others.

The purpose of Exercise 2 is to highlight that Emily's request for help with overcoming low self-esteem is not one to which you can immediately respond. Rather, her account of her difficulties provokes a series of further questions to which you need answers in order to identify a meaningful way forward. Each question you ask, each hypothesis you develop, is based on some prior reasoning about what might be relevant to explore further. In other words, from the earliest stages of your encounter with the client, you cannot help but make decisions.

Diverse theories about how to create change, specific techniques, knowledge of the available evidence and professional and ethical guidelines all need to come together with learning how to listen to clients' stories to form effective, collaborative therapeutic relationships. It is a daunting task and any trainee therapist will be acutely aware of wanting to be empowering, effective and ethical in their service offer, yet at the same time having to work with considerable amounts of uncertainty and ambiguity.

Not surprisingly, faced with so many competing tasks, the quest for certainty can become very seductive. We feel compelled to minimize uncertainty, want concrete guidance on what to do and when, and hope that our supervisors, trainers, articles and books will provide clear-cut answers – what Scaturo and McPeak (1998) refer to as 'cook books' – to the endless series of questions to which our professional practice gives rise.

A desire for prescriptions may be understandable and treatment protocols that offer substantive advice on what to do when can be highly valuable when used wisely. However, they cannot protect us from the ambiguities that are inherent in professional practice. As Leahy (2003) points out, the gaps in what we need to learn tend to outweigh what we have learned so far, even for very experienced practitioners.

It is perhaps reassuring to learn that uncertainty is not necessarily a sign of incompetence! Nonetheless, if we acknowledge that the way in which we approach our work with a client, based on the questions we ask, will inevitably close down some options even while opening up others, it follows that we must be very clear about what is informing our choices and whether those choices are based on an accurate appraisal of the information available to us. This gives rise to important questions, including the following:

- How can I know if my decisions are accurate?
- How would other therapists and/or colleagues judge my decision in this situation? Would they see my judgement here as valid or questionable?
- How do I imagine that my decision in this situation would compare with that of an expert in this field?
- Does a treatment protocol exist for this client's presenting problem? If so, how does my decision-making compare with what might be advocated as the optimum way forward? Am I making decisions in ways that would be consistent with, or in contrast to, current thinking or treatment protocols in this area?

To help us consider these questions, we now turn our attention to some of the attempts that have been made to investigate practitioners' decision-making and examine what these approaches might tell us about the quality of our thinking skills. We are exploring this literature so that you can consider how important accuracy is to your practice and what might get in the way of being accurate in your decisions with clients.

A critical review of our decision-making abilities: just how accurate are we?

Practitioners' decision-making ability has been a subject of academic interest since the 1950s, and the field now boasts a wide range of studies examining the extent to which our claims to expertise are as valid as we might publicly proclaim (Gambrill 2005). A review of the literature highlights a wide range of approaches to investigating practitioners' judgements that span comparisons of judgement accuracy between trained clinicians and non-trained individuals, examining the effects of experience on decision-making ability and the relative impact of different sources of influence on decisions made.

An important point to note here is the nature of the research methodology that has informed much of this literature. Specifically, a characteristic of these early studies is the emphasis on examining how clinical judge-ments fared against statistical predictions. This approach makes sense when we consider the way in which our primary responsibilities to clients have often been conceptualized. For example, O'Donohue and Henderson (1999) proposed that we have four principle responsibilities:

1. We must be current with regard to the knowledge status of the field as this relates to a client's presenting problem.
2. We must make accurate and relevant judgements about this knowledge.
3. We must be aware of our personal limitations in training and experience.
4. We must accurately and effectively communicate this knowledge to the client.

What underpins these principles is a belief that accuracy is equated with responsibility. Indeed, O'Donohue and Henderson (1999) elevate these principles to the status of an 'ethical and epistemic duty'. They argue that as therapists, we have a responsibility to acquire knowledge – this is our *epistemic* duty to our clients. Our *ethical* duty comes in applying this knowledge accurately. They make the case that the public expects to be able to receive specialist knowledge and skills and that when we resort to intuition or anecdotes we are in fact doing our clients a great disservice and failing in our obligations to them. Thus, we must maintain *accurate* (up-to-date) knowledge; we must be *accurate* in our understanding of this knowledge; we must be able to *accurately* assess our own level of competence and we must be able to *accurately* communicate knowledge to clients in ways they can understand. From this argument it would appear that we need to be accurate in our decisions. However, in practice this may not always be easy to achieve.

Unfortunately for a profession which claims to be based on a system-atic approach to enquiry, the results from a number of studies make for uncomfortable reading. It would appear that:

- there is little relationship between training and judgement (Oskamp 1965; Carkhuf and Berenson 1967);
- therapists may not use any systematic decision process at all (O'Donohue et al. 1990);
- many practitioners rely more on personal experience than the decision-making literature (Turk and Salovey 1985);
- clinicians rely on a large number of anecdotal impressions to form judgements (Meehl 1997);

- negative attitudes towards research have persisted and continue to represent a barrier to the dissemination of evidence-based psychological treatments (Shafran et al. 2009);
- there is under-estimation of the importance of specific protocols in determining outcomes and over-estimation of the influence of the therapeutic relationship (Shafran et al. 2009).

This reads very negatively and of course not all studies have yielded such disappointing conclusions. In decision-making in cognitive case formulation, for example, Bieling and Kuyken (2003) show reasonable levels of agreement between practitioners in defining the actual features of a client's presenting difficulties (the descriptive level), although that agreement becomes modest when practitioners seek to identify relevant psychological mechanisms and underlying cognitions (the interpretive level). Yet Luborsky and Crits-Cristoph (1990) have shown that using a structured process of eliciting core conflictual relationship themes does produce reliable measures. Turpin (2001) has argued that the use of baseline and repeated measures can also improve decision-making. In all cases there is a need to respect the limitations of the data and not seek interpretations beyond it.

Taken as a whole, the literature does not generate confidence in the accuracy of our judgements. This would appear to lend support to O'Donohue and Henderson's (1999) claim that in the main, practitioners have scant awareness of the factors that influence their judgements, and Meehl's (1997) argument that as professional practitioners we must be clearer about the basis for the knowledge claims we make. So if our decision-making is not always as accurate as we might like to believe, what gets in the way? Are we really bad at what we do? Is this literature over-stating the 'accuracy argument'? Or are there common biases that get in the way? This is considered next.

What inhibits accurate decision-making: insights from the literature

A number of authors have attempted to catalogue the types of error that may interfere with the accuracy of our decision-making. In reviewing a wide range of studies, Sterman (1994) identifies a number of barriers, including the inevitable limitations of human cognitive processes, misperceptions of feedback, dilemmas that arise from having to manage ambiguity and confounding variables, and the tendency to stop looking once a single causative link has been found. He concludes that neither scientists nor professionals are immune to these influences; there are, it seems, common problems that we need to address.

From the perspective of cognitive psychology, Arkes (1981) identified five impediments to accurate judgement:

- co-variation (which Arkes argues we tend to underestimate);
- preconceived notions about a client's needs that 'warp' our perception of incoming data and lead us to infer relationships between factors that do not actually exist;
- lack of awareness of the factors that actually influence our judgements;
- overconfidence in our diagnostic and treatment capability;
- the hindsight bias.

These types of biases were echoed by the later work of O'Donohue and Henderson (1999) who warn against the following types of errors:

- false descriptive statements;
- false causal statements;
- false ontic statements (where we think that things exist when they do not);
- false relational claims;
- false predictions;
- false professional ethical claims (believing it is acceptable to engage in certain types of behaviours with clients, when it is not).

Some examples might illustrate these biases at work, and the ease with which we might become prone to them. For example, the bias of holding the preconceived notion that a client's difficulties are the result of traumatic early experiences might prevent a therapist from seeking out information that alerts us to powerful maintaining factors in the here and now. Equally, an attachment to models of therapy that construe difficulties as arising from cognitive biases might prevent a therapist from asking about the client's circumstances that could reveal the presence of disempowering environmental factors, with the potential to make a false causal statement. Overconfidence in the accuracy of our judgements might lead us to offer solutions to clients prematurely before sufficient understanding of their circumstances and needs has been obtained.

Arkes (1981) also highlights the ease with which we can assume that positive change in a client's life is a direct result of the intervention we have provided, rather than other types of influence, particularly given the tendency of practitioners to selectively seek evidence that confirms their hypotheses and disregard evidence that contradicts their judgements (Koriat et al. 1980). As Arkes (1981: 326) reminds us, the hindsight bias ensures that there is 'always enough evidence in a rich source of data to nurture all but the most outlandish diagnosis'. We tend to see what we expect or want to see.

It is important to note that these types of influence can operate very subtly and some of these biases may be more easily accessible to conscious awareness than others. It would be incorrect, therefore, to assume that the presence of these biases solely affects those engaged in what we might obviously judge as ineffective or unethical practice (indeed, this might be an example of the 'lack of awareness' bias that Arkes identifies!). Rather, they have the potential to affect us all and it is important to evaluate our practice in light of these widely identified biases and to consider ways in which we might counteract them.

Exercise 3: *Which biases tend to operate in your thinking?*

Impediments to accurate decision-making affect all of us, no matter how experienced we are as therapists. Reflecting on the impediments to accurate judgement identified in the literature, think about your own approach to making decisions – in therapy and more generally. Which types of error tend to characterize your decision-making? Can you think of an example from your own life where this occurred?

If accuracy is an important part of our service offer, then we need to find ways to improve it. In the next section, we offer three possibilities for doing so.

Useful frameworks for improving the accuracy of your decision-making

The literature which has attempted to identify and catalogue the different types of thinking bias is extremely valuable in increasing our awareness and helping us consider ways of improving the accuracy of our decision-making. Although Arkes (1981) argued that there is little point in providing information on specific biases because this does not counteract the 'lack of awareness' bias, others have painted a more optimistic picture of how the accuracy of practitioners' judgements can be improved through education. For example, Chen et al. (1997) found that instruction in attribution processes enabled trainee counsellors to reduce such biases. Round (1999) also found that providing explicit instruction in decision-making processes and the biases that can occur had a beneficial effect on the accuracy of decisions made by fourth-year medical students. By raising awareness of potential impediments to accuracy it may, therefore, become possible to take steps to correct them. In the service of this aim, three frameworks drawn from different branches of psychology may be particularly helpful: attribution theory, heuristics and information-processing theory.

Attribution theory

Attribution theory has an important contribution to make to the study of practitioners' decision-making. In essence, it is concerned with how individuals interpret events and how these interpretations shape subsequent thinking and action. It is based on the assumption that human beings are motivated to make sense of why people act in the way that they do. Heider (1958) proposed that attributions fall into one of two categories: *internal*, the inference being that a person is behaving in a particular way because of some quality or characteristic they possess, such as a personality trait, moral code, or belief; and *external*, the inference being that a person is behaving in a particular way because of situational factors that are essentially beyond the person's control. Where an internal attribution is made, the individual is considered to be in control of, or responsible for, the outcome. Where an external attribution is applied, the event is deemed to be responsible for the individual's behaviour.

Subsequent theoretical elaborations were proposed by Kelley (1967), who emphasized explanations of behaviour as including the dimensions of person, entity and time, and Weiner et al. (1971), who incorporated stable and variable causes. Brewin (1989) provided an application in counselling psychology and, in particular, considered how people use attributions as decision rules to label their emotions and then search for causes.

Attribution theory has significant implications for us as therapists. In the context of therapeutic decision-making, it encourages us to improve the effectiveness of clinical interventions through understanding how both clients and therapists attribute causes to the client's behaviour. Försterling (1988) suggests that attention to attributions enables practitioners to respond to the clients' clinical needs while also appealing to their belief systems.

Exercise 4:   *What kind of causal analyst are you?*

According to attribution theory, we operate as *causal analysts*, inferring the characteristics of a person through our perceptions of them. In a study investigating how practitioners explain the successes and failures in their practice, it was found that success tended to be attributed to internal stable factors ('I am a good therapist') while failure was attributed to external, uncontrollable factors ('The client's circumstances changed which made it difficult for her to benefit from therapy'; see Curtis 1994).

Identify a situation, piece of work with a client or other project where you achieved the outcome you had hoped for – preferably a professional one. Consider how you explained:

- the cause of the (client's) problem;
- the outcome;
- your own and others' (or the client's) contribution to the outcome.

Now identify a situation, piece of work with a client or other project where you did not get the outcome you had hoped for – preferably a professional one. Consider how you explained:

- the cause of the (client's) problem;
- the outcome;
- your own and others' (or the client's) contribution to the outcome.

What can you learn from this about your own style of attribution?

Heuristics

Another framework that helps explain how we arrive at some (less accurate) judgements over others is to consider the role of heuristics. In their influential work, Tversky and Kahneman (1973, 1974; Kahneman et al. 1982) highlight how the efficient processing of information is dependent upon the use of cognitive strategies or decision-making rules known as heuristics. Heuristics enable us to reduce complex aspects of the decision-making process to more manageable components so we can make inferences in systematic ways.

In their research into the effects of heuristics on the accuracy of clinical judgement Tversky and Kahneman (1973, 1974) identify three specific heuristics that are commonly employed. These are:

- the *availability* heuristic, whereby estimations of frequency, probability or causality vary according to the extent to which they are 'available' in memory;
- the *representativeness* heuristic, whereby objects or people are categorized according to their perceived similarity to a prototype;
- the *anchoring* heuristic, referring to a tendency to retain our beliefs in the light of new information that disconfirms them.

We should also be aware of two additional decision-making short-cuts:

- the *confirmatory bias*, that is, the tendency to seek out information which confirms our hypotheses. From the perspective of applied psychology, this includes how preconceptions stemming from training or preferred theoretical orientation shape what we actually observe (Lord et al. 1979; Turk and Salovey 1985).
- the *illusory correlation*, namely perceiving causal relationships where none exist (Tversky and Kahneman 1980; O'Donohue and Henderson 1999).

Because heuristics enable us to organize often large amounts of information swiftly and efficiently, they are useful in many situations. However, they can also lead to systematic reasoning biases that prove problematic in situations where accuracy (rather than efficiency) is required.

Exercise 5: *Correcting a heuristic error. What would you do?*

A newly qualified therapist had recently attended a workshop on how to support clients who have experienced child sexual abuse. This included some of the indicators that a therapist might be attentive to in the early stages of therapy. With this information at the forefront of his mind, the following week the therapist assessed a female client who appeared anxious in the session and seemed reticent about discussing her relationship with her father which she described as 'difficult'. The client reported feeling uncomfortable in social situations, and was requesting help with this. She was particularly anxious in meetings at work, where she often had to give presentations to senior (exclusively male) members of the company. She denied having experienced sexual abuse as a child but admitted to feeling anxious in the presence of male authority figures.

Based on her presentation and reaction to him, and the information he had acquired from the workshop, the therapist developed a hypothesis that the client had been sexually abused but that the client was not ready to disclose this. Following discussion, the supervisor commented that while this was a potentially valid hypothesis, there was as yet no evidence to support it and it was important for the therapist to explore other avenues, including whether the client was experiencing difficulties consistent with social anxiety.

At the next supervision session, the therapist presented further 'evidence' that the client had been sexually abused (which his supervisor thought was of dubious credibility) and continued to probe for confirmation from the client that she had been sexually abused. He had not yet explored whether or not she might be experiencing the types of difficulty characteristic typical of social anxiety.

Which heuristic(s) might be operating here? If you were supervising this therapist, how would you encourage him to take a broader view?

Schemas and cognitive distortions

It has been proposed that we all operate with implicit personality theories which guide recall of events (e.g. Shweder 1977). A more recent attempt to understand these implicit personality theories and their role in the actions and decisions of therapists has come from Witteman and Koele (1999) who suggest that through the process of counselling or psychotherapy training, we acquire a 'schema' that concerns the type of client or client difficulty that may be helped by the skills we have developed. They propose that as we acquire more methods for working with clients, our schema becomes elaborated but that we nonetheless continue to work within our schematic range. If a particular client's concern provides a match with our schema, we draw on that schema to justify our choice of intervention. If, however, no match is found, we are more likely to refer the client elsewhere. They argue that this can account for some of the decision-making procedures we follow – it is not so much the client characteristics or the therapist's theoretical background that determines the choice made, but rather the schema that informs the decision.

The concept of schema has been important for psychotherapists and a particular focus of cognitive (Beck et al. 1979) and schema-focused (Young 1994) therapies. Within cognitive therapy perceptual and interpretive biases, filtered through our schema (the cognitive structures in the mind), are deemed central to understanding human distress and developing effective interventions. Influenced by the Stoic philosopher, Epictetus, who advocated that people are disturbed not by events but the views they take of them, cognitive therapists would advocate that emotional difficulties are mediated and maintained by biased, unrealistic interpretations of events that contradict the evidence. In essence, the client's difficulties are understood as being maintained by faulty information processing which can be identified, re-examined and revised in the light of the available evidence.

In schema therapy the focus is on the implicit, unconditional and taken-for-granted 'truths' that individuals have acquired. Those schemas that are the target of therapeutic intervention comprise a network of memories, emotions, cognitions and sensations. They are believed to develop early in life, in an attempt to help the person make sense of their experiences and avoid further pain. They are elaborated over the years and form the basis for interpreting events in adulthood when they are no longer relevant, appropriate or helpful. In this sense, they are dysfunctional.

Young (1994), in particular, has focused on identifying and modifying those schemas that are the product of toxic childhood experiences with parents, siblings and peers – termed *early maladaptive schemas* – which represent broad, pervasive themes regarding oneself, others and the world. Schemas tend to be self-sustaining and persist even in the face of disconfirmatory evidence. This is particularly the case for early maladaptive schemas which are typically highly rigid and resistant to modification.

Exercise 6:   *What are your therapy schemas?*

Witteman and Koele (1999) propose that many of our therapy-related decisions are 'schema-driven' and in support of this cite research that the more experienced we are in a certain task, the less explicit and elaborate our decision-making processes become.

The notion that our decisions as therapists are schema-driven enables us to think about ways in which we might become stuck in styles of thinking that prevent us from responding optimally to our client's needs. Consider those deeply held beliefs, or schemas, that you have in relation to each of the following areas:

- people as clients (e.g. strong/vulnerable; healthy/disturbed; resourceful/non-resourceful; trustworthy/untrustworthy; capable of self-direction/requiring direction; capable/incapable of change);

- people as therapists (client has responsibility for change/ therapist has responsibility for change; therapist as educator/ healer/clinician, etc.);
- therapy as a change process (treatment/journey of discovery; guided/directed; exploration/education);
- the nature of clients' presenting problems (diagnosable disorders/problems in living; sign of pathology/sign of living; views on human nature, etc.).

While schemas represent those deeply held networks of belief that guide how we operate, often at a partial level of conscious awareness, cognitive theory suggests that our stream of consciously accessible thoughts, represented in our moment-to-moment experience of events, can also be influenced by particular perceptual and interpretive biases. Such biases are particularly prevalent when we are feeling emotionally challenged in some way. There are a wide range of these reported in the literature and Corrie (2009) provides a useful summary. Some of the most common include cognitive distortions such as:

- over-generalizing from data (i.e. making sweeping, generalized conclusions based on a single event, such as where a person has a minor setback and concludes, 'Things *never* work out for me. Sooner or later, it *always* goes wrong. I might as well not bother';
- seeing things in dichotomous (all-or-nothing) terms (viewing situations and events from extreme perspectives with no middle ground, such as 'If I don't get a distinction on every piece of work, it means I'm a total failure');
- catastrophizing (exaggerating greatly the significance of an event, e.g. 'If I make a mistake on this project, others will realize that I'm a failure, my partner will leave me, I'll lose my job, won't be able to pay the mortgage and will end up homeless');
- labelling (you sum up yourself or others in a single, usually critical or judgemental word, e.g. 'I am stupid'; 'I am a failure' – this is often an extreme form of all-or-nothing thinking);
- emotional reasoning (believing things are true because they feel true, rather than basing your judgement on an impartial evaluation of the situation).

Cognitive distortions can bias our decision-making and problem-solving skills in a variety of ways, including in relation to how we access and use the knowledge of our discipline. Gambrill (2005), for example, describes a 'false belief' typical of a number of therapists that drawing on practice-related research does not allow practitioners to exercise their individual creativity or judgement – a cognitive distortion we could interpret as containing elements of dichotomous thinking.

As these thinking traps have been identified as normal aspects of human thinking, it is highly likely that you engage in some of them at least some of the time. It is useful to think about your own 'profile' of favoured distortions in different situations and how you might counter these. For example, which tend to operate when you are feeling overworked? Facing an impending deadline? Unsettled by a client's reactions to you in a session? When you fail a college assignment or receive critical feedback? Equally, what is different about how you judge yourself and your skills when you feel very effective in your practice? When progress with a client seems to be very smooth? When you are praised for the quality of your work? When you find yourself developing strong feelings of attachment to a particular client? You might find it helpful to discuss these with your supervisor so you can be attentive to their emergence and take steps to ensure that they do not interfere with your therapeutic decision-making.

Sarah's log

One hot summer's day, with the window behind me wide open to allow a gentle breeze into the consulting room, I was working with a client (whom I shall call 'Bill') on his experience of depression. We had been discussing the ways in which cognitive distortions can exert an unhelpful influence on a person's reactions and how this idea might be relevant to Bill's needs.

As we talked, I noticed that Bill seemed distracted by something occurring over my shoulder. 'By the way,' he said, 'I hope you don't mind spiders, because there's a *really large* one on the window sill behind you'. As someone who had (almost) overcome their fear of large spiders, I felt myself freeze.

'Do you want me to put it outside for you?' Bill asked kindly, observing my obvious paralysis. I nodded and after taking a deep breath, turned around to face what was nothing more than an average sized spider that I would normally have dealt with without a second thought. But I still felt frozen to the spot. Bill's comment had led me to imagine a spider that spanned two foot in diameter heading purposefully towards me with malicious intent. And even though my eyes told me one thing, the image in my mind overrode my logical reasoning.

When we returned to the focus of our session (the spider safely restored to its natural habitat), Bill told me that although it certainly hadn't been a planned experiment, it was the best illustration I could have given him of how cognitive distortions can affect a person's behaviour!

Can you identify what cognitive distortions might have been operating for me in this scenario? How would you have helped me correct this (these) distortion(s)?

Specific steps you can take to improve the accuracy of your decision-making

In this chapter, we have reviewed the literature which highlights the importance of accurate decision-making. We have considered three important frameworks that can help you increase the accuracy of your decisions: attribution theory, heuristics, and cognitive processing in the form of schemas and cognitive distortions. Here are some additional steps you can take:

- Practice identifying what is really driving your judgements and decisions in each case. In the spirit of Meehl, ask yourself 'What is the basis for the knowledge claims I am making with this client, in this session?' Be very honest about how much you are relying on scientific principles, state-of-the-art knowledge, intuition, past practice or some other factor.
- Be humble! Recognize that your current ideas might be wrong and incorporate a 'falsificationist' mindset into your work. This involves being clear about the circumstances in which you would be prepared to abandon a pet theory or belief about a client's needs and take a fresh look. Knowing when to let go of a favoured hunch or hypothesis is a critical component of improving accuracy.
- Be inclusive, particularly early on in your work with a client. Generate as many hypotheses about a client's circumstances, difficulties and needs as you can and gather information to test all of them until a clearer picture begins to emerge.
- Remember, the more convinced you are that a hypothesis is correct, the more cautious you want to be, as there could be a cognitive distortion operating!
- Audio- or video-record a session and go through this in detail, identifying the decisions that sat behind each of your comments

and reactions. Discuss these with your supervisor or trainer for feedback.

- Be aware of your own profile of cognitive distortions. Become skilled at recognizing the presence of these biases and take steps to correct them (for an example of how to do this, see Corrie 2009).

Exercise 7: *Analysing a decision that proved to be unhelpful*

Go back to the exercise you completed in the Introduction to this book (Exercise 1). Focus on the decision that did not bring about the result you wanted. Looking back at what occurred in light of the models discussed in this chapter, can you identity any attributions that you made that may have contributed to this result? What heuristics might have been operating? Could any cognitive distortions have clouded your thinking? In hindsight, what did these attributions, heuristics or distortions lead you to conclude, or prevent you from seeing, and how did they influence what happened next?

Make a note of any relevant themes in your learning log and give some thought to how you could monitor these in the future, to prevent you from falling into a similar trap. You might also like to discuss these with your supervisor, trainer or colleagues for further guidance.

Conclusion

The purpose of this chapter has been to raise your awareness of, and help you assess, your decision-making approach, become familiar with some of the principal errors in decision-making to which you might be prone, and offer methods for helping you overcome these biases. Although it is never possible to eradicate decision-making biases, it is possible – and indeed extremely important – to be aware of when you are taking cognitive short-cuts and whether you are aware of the potential implications of having done so. It is not about losing heart in our abilities, but rather being aware of bias and preparing for it.

What is so helpful about this literature is that it encourages an attitude of appropriate caution and humility in relation to our decisions. It calls upon us to examine what is really influencing our judgements in different situations and reminds us that, if we are less than satisfied with what we discover, we are not alone and should feel confident about raising such dilemmas in supervision and in team meetings, because our colleagues are likely to be just as affected by these biases as are we.

However, there is another side to the debate. A number of researchers have argued that the focus on accuracy that has dominated so much of the literature has failed to capture the richness of the mental operations that are required of therapists when working with their clients. This raises an interesting counter-argument that encourages us to identify the wider range of thinking, problem-solving and reasoning skills that effective therapy requires.

As Kwiatkowski and Winter (2006) observe, practitioners have to exist in several worlds simultaneously. There are always multiple decisions to be made and numerous courses of action that may be helpful, and in such situations a decision-making literature that focuses exclusively on accuracy is not necessarily as helpful or as illuminating as it might initially appear. We will be asking you later, when you come to build your decision-making model, to think of the contexts that make accuracy vital and those that make it insufficient to address the needs of the client in front of you.

We will examine these important counter-arguments, and consider their implications for practice, in Chapter 2. But before we do, we would invite you to conclude Chapter 1 by using the learning summary box below. What, for you, has stood out from this chapter and what would you like to take forward with you for further discussion, reflection or active experimentation?

✍ Learning summary

One idea I have found useful in this chapter is. . .

. . . .

. . . .

One thing I would like to experiment with, having read this chapter, is. . .

. . . .

. . . .

Was there anything I didn't quite understand? (If so, I will find out more by. . .)

. . . .

. . . .

2 Beyond the question of accuracy: Decision-making in the real world

---

In this chapter you will learn about:

- the types of reasoning skills that are needed by practitioners
- the debates on how we should investigate therapists' decision-making
- the implications of these debates for therapy practice

By reading this chapter you will be able to:

- understand the frameworks of reasoning that are needed in practice
- consider the contexts in your practice that make accuracy insufficient
- consider when something other than accuracy needs to drive the investigation

---

Introduction

In the previous chapter we examined the literature which has attempted to investigate the accuracy of practitioners' decision-making and clinical judgement. While our official rhetoric emphasizes that our decisions are the product of rational criteria, logically applied, the research literature suggests that our decisions are all too often characterized by inconsistency and bias. But how should we make sense of this? Should we assume that therapists' decisions are so inaccurate that their thinking is inherently untrustworthy? And if this is the case, what basis do we have for offering our services to the public?

In this chapter, we take a closer look at the assumptions that underpin much of this literature and examine what can, and cannot, be concluded from its findings. We begin by considering some areas of controversy and then make the case that while accuracy is an important aspect of knowing whether our decisions are sound, it is far from being the whole story. In particular, we propose that any attempts to improve the accuracy of our decisions should be considered alongside an appreciation of the range of mental operations and reasoning skills that practitioners need to function as effective therapists.

The quest for accuracy as a 'foundational belief'

Chapter 1 highlighted the need to be cautious about the degree of confidence we place in our decisions. However, to gain a truly accurate picture of therapists' decision-making prowess, we must also consider the nature of the research used to investigate it. The studies reviewed in Chapter 1 are largely based on the assumption that decision-making is, or should be, rational and logical. Rationality and logic are so highly regarded in western culture, and so closely associated with notions of credibility and quality, that we can forget that this, too, is a belief rather than a fact. Mahrer (2000) uses the term *foundational assumption* to describe those beliefs that over time become so deeply entrenched, so central to how we think and act, that we forget to question them. The idea that accuracy equates to quality is one such foundational assumption, but there are many others.

> ### Exercise 8:   *What foundational beliefs underpin therapy?*
>
> Take a moment to think about the fields of counselling and psychotherapy. Based on your experience so far (including books and articles you have read, any teaching you have experienced, your own practice and experience of being a client in therapy), what would you see as some of the foundational assumptions that characterize the fields of counselling and psychotherapy at this time? List them in your learning log.

We are not suggesting that our foundational assumptions are necessarily wrong, but rather that it is important to evaluate them so that we might become more aware of how they influence our work with clients. By becoming increasingly aware of the assumptions that we might have uncritically adopted due to the culture, context and historical period in which we are living and working, we are potentially better placed to consider those that are helpful and those that are less so. Indeed, Mahrer has challenged psychology to identify and deconstruct its foundational beliefs in order to develop a greater collective understanding of the basis of our knowledge claims and how our beliefs might impact on our clients, for good or ill. So let us now consider the kind of methodologies to which this foundational belief – that our decision-making must be rational and logical to be credible – has given rise.

Taking a closer look at the literature

We could consider the emphasis on accuracy (which is reflected in much of the literature that has investigated practitioners' decision-making abilities to date) as being a foundational belief to which psychotherapy and psychology have uncritically adhered. Many of these studies (explicitly or implicitly) are underpinned by an *information-processing framework* (Ivey et al. 1999).

In essence, the information-processing framework draws on a conceptual model which views decisions as progressing through a series of logical, rational and sequential stages whereby data received from the environment are processed systematically to arrive at a mental representation of some aspect of the external world.

This approach to decision-making is illustrated in another genre that is very popular in contemporary western culture, namely, the murder mystery. Here, the style of reasoning needed to solve the crime involves an approach to problem-solving that follows a clear-cut sequence as outlined below:

Stage 1: A crime has been committed. (The problem is unambiguous from the outset.)

Stage 2: The crime must be solved and the perpetrator discovered. (The task to be undertaken, in this case by a detective, is equally unambiguous.)

Stage 3: A specific process must be followed to achieve this outcome. The crime is solved through gathering evidence, forming hypotheses and gathering more evidence to confirm or disconfirm the various hypotheses, leading to a clear understanding of the facts.

Stage 4: The perpetrator is identified and so the crime is solved.

It is important to note that there can be no room for manoeuvre in this sequence – both the nature of the problem (the crime) and the desirable outcome (the solving of the crime) are pre-determined. While there may be some sequential variations – the crime is at first incorrectly classified as an accident, or the perpetrator was motivated by circumstances which prevent us from unconditionally vilifying their character – the decision-making scenario has been decided from the outset, due to the structure imposed upon it. The structure provides the framework that gives meaning to each character's actions and motivations, and it is the framework that determines how the story unfolds. For example, the murder mystery would not 'work' if the crime suddenly became irrelevant and the story 'genre' switched mid-way through to a romance (for a more detailed analysis of story motifs and their relevance to therapy, see Corrie and Lane 2010). In the murder mystery, the outcome of the detective work will either be accurate or inaccurate, as a function of the quality of the data-gathering and the interpretation of the data along the way.

To make the link explicit, what both the detective story and the information-processing approach to therapists' decision-making share is a concern with the 'output' of the process in the form of the accuracy of the judgement made (Siegert 1999). An accurate decision is a good decision, whereas an inaccurate decision is a bad decision. And ultimately, there is only one correct answer.

Once we view therapists' decision-making through the lens of this formula, certain consequences follow. One consequence is that it becomes legitimate to compare practitioners' *actual* decisions with how they *should* make decisions. Studies based on the information-processing approach take as a starting point that there is a correct answer. They then seek to determine how practitioners' decisions measure up or fall short. As a result, it follows that an effective way to investigate professionals' judgements is through use of methods that are generally regarded as 'objective', enabling a point of comparison. Accordingly, the dominance of the information-processing model has resulted in a range of methods that examine how professional judgements compare with the rigorous and objective approach of statistical (or actuarial) prediction (Meehl 1954, 1957; Dowie and Elstein 1988). However, it is here that we start to encounter problems.

Grounding the research in the challenges that therapists encounter

The worlds of counselling and psychotherapy rarely present us with clear-cut problems, let alone dilemmas to which there can be any single, correct answer. As we have noted elsewhere (see Lane and Corrie 2006), the problems with which practitioners are generally concerned are often ill structured and ill defined, and in the early stages of working with a client it is not uncommon for the therapist to have to 'assemble' clients' difficulties from an array of conflicting pieces of information and competing demands and priorities. Indeed, one of the hallmarks of experience could be said to be learning to identify what is most salient in a client's presentation.

Additionally, in therapy practice, there are always multiple decisions to be made and potentially numerous courses of action that may be helpful. Equally, our decisions tend to be relative rather than absolute and must be interpreted in the light of the most compelling factors facing us at that time. This might be crisis intervention, pressures to manage waiting lists more effectively, or the extent to which an offer of service is acceptable to the client (Sobell and Sobell 2000), to name but a few.

A quality service, then, comprises something more nuanced than the extent to which decisions are accurate. Accuracy is a vital skill, but it takes its place among a broader set of reasoning skills that inform our response to a particular situation. For example, the capacity to accurately assess whether or not a post-natally depressed woman is at risk of harming herself or her baby is essential to working safely and effectively with the client and those, such as her baby, who might be impacted by her difficulties. Equally, if we are aware of the evidence that suggests that imaginal reliving is an effective treatment for specific symptoms of post-traumatic stress disorder, we need to be able to accurately assess whether or not our client meets these diagnostic criteria as a precursor to offering this type of intervention.

However, if we want to make a decision about how best to introduce a client to a new idea (such as the cognitive distortions described in Chapter 1) we need a different type of thinking skill. Here we might be concerned with devising a creative illustration that will enable the client to consider the relevance of these ideas to their own situation. So we might simply present the client with a list of the different distortions, consider using a story, or use an analogy that connects to something meaningful in the client's life, such as a professional role or a hobby. Alternatively, we might proceed based on our understanding of how the client learns best. We might even be able to take advantage of an unexpected occurrence, as Sarah's spider reaction (described in Chapter 1) demonstrates!

Consider the following case vignettes. In each case the client presented with mild depression. In devising an intervention plan, certain decisions had to be made concerning the style of approach that would be most likely to engage the client. How would you have proceeded if Jenny and Vivienne had been your clients?

Client 1: Jenny

For Jenny, achieving targets was a naturally occurring reinforcer. Once they had agreed to work together, Jenny and her therapist spent time identifying an approach to target setting that also took account of some of the difficulties imposed by her depression – in particular, impaired memory functioning and loss of energy. Jenny decided that she would like to audio-record her therapy sessions to listen to between sessions (one of her weekly targets which also helped her manage her memory difficulties). Additionally, at the end of each meeting, she thought it would be helpful to identify two target behaviours (starting small and building up to more ambitious steps over time) for the week ahead.

Jenny said that this plan of action gave her a sense of hope and optimism. However, her therapist was also aware that Jenny tended to be highly driven and at times could expect too much of herself – a pattern which was implicated in the onset of her depression. Having discussed this, they agreed to monitor the impact of setting weekly targets to see whether or not it delivered the results that Jenny expected. Nonetheless, during the planning phase, her therapist came to understand how setting targets was typical of Jenny's approach during the times that she had felt most effective in her life and represented an important skill that could be used to help her manage the depression more effectively.

Client 2: Vivienne

Vivienne valued the opportunity to reflect on her own story, sifting through different events and her reactions to them to search for common narrative threads. As she described it, 'What really helps me is being able to make sense of how it all pieces together'. Understanding her depression, and documenting her reflections through keeping a diary, was extremely valuable to her and in keeping with her style of self-expression. Vivienne told her therapist that story-telling was a way of learning that fostered her self-reflective capabilities, and she anticipated that finding ways to connect with this natural preference would pave the way for positive emotional change. Exploring this further, and agreeing to test out the approach to see how it worked for her, Vivienne and her therapist discovered that it did not result in unhelpful rumination (which can easily occur in depression), but enabled her to connect with something important inside of herself that she identified as her 'authentic voice'. Again, this was consistent with how she had learned best at other times in her life.

In these two examples, the approach chosen to facilitate change was congruent with the needs, learning style and preferences of the client. To have overlooked these preferences in favour of focusing on the client's symptom profile might have risked alienating the client in both cases. However, these kinds of choices, while carefully made, did not rely predominantly on criteria relating to accuracy.

In consequence, questions of accuracy may become less pressing when the task is deciding how best to engage a client, how to uncover new possibilities and how to design a way forward. Here, we may find ourselves relying more on ideas generated about the client's preferred approach to learning, their interpersonal style and their values. These are likely to be informed by the therapist's sensitivity to an amalgam of non-verbal cues, initial reactions to questions or moments of silence and the client's statements about what is easy and difficult about the experience of being in therapy. However, it is unlikely that viewing these choices through the lens of increasing accuracy will enable the therapist to generate improvements in their practice. As such, the information-processing approach with its emphasis on linear and sequential decision-making falls short of what is required.

Beyond matters of accuracy: what do we know about how therapists make decisions?

Scaturo and McPeak (1998: 1) describe professional practice as 'a constant series of clinical choices and recurring sets of dilemmas'. Psychological practice is a complex human arena. This is partly because in therapy the individuals and systems on whose behalf we are attempting to intervene are constantly evolving, rather than static entities (Hogarth 1981). This recognition has given rise to a growing appreciation that therapists' decisions are not isolated cognitive events or 'outputs' that can be understood as objectively correct or incorrect, but rather cognitive events whose value must be interpreted in relation to a particular task at a particular point in time; all our decisions are relative (Dowie and Elstein 1988). Once we attempt to look at decision-making outside of the context in which it occurs, we are in danger of arriving at a distorted and misleading picture of clinical judgement in the work place. This has led to a number of attempts by researchers to understand how practitioners *actually* make decisions, rather than how their judgements fare in statistical studies of reliability.

Edwards (2002; cited as below in Lane and Corrie 2006) identified a range of factors that were central to how clinical psychologists viewed their own decision-making processes during therapy assessments. She identified nine main themes relating to the following:

- The framing of the assessment, comprising psychologists' own needs, the impact of service factors and the preconceived ideas of the client.
- What the psychologist is likely to do, in terms of typical ways of working and prior openness to treatment decisions. This would seem to be consistent with Witteman and Kunst's (1999) finding that therapists' preferred way of working typically represented the starting point of an investigation, rather than a detailed description of the case. Factors such as time constraints, availability of therapists, and preferences for certain types of clients influence the decisions made in critical ways.
- Exploring and responding to the 'fit', including the fit between the psychologist and the client, assessing clients' issues, the client's ability to work with certain modalities and treatment decisions. This perhaps fits with Seidenstücker and Roth's (1998) argument that practitioners do not necessarily decide on an approach based on the data available to them but evolve their stance through working with a particular client over time.

The themes identified highlight that choices are context-dependent, shaped by individual values, and by the need to develop ways of facilitating decision-making that serve our purpose in the context of a given client enquiry.

The recognition that our choices are context-dependent has given rise to a number of attempts to improve our reasoning skills 'in action'. These include verbalizing the process of decision-making, thus enabling reflection and critique as well as sharing the process with and teaching it to other therapists (Crabtree 1998), and the introduction of manualized and protocol-driven approaches which essentially reduce the decision-making process to component parts through providing a menu of options at different stages.

Protocols may have particular benefits for enhancing our reasoning skills when the issue to be addressed is clear and undisputed. They provide a way of uniting professional judgement with research evidence and can foster cohesive team working by organizing members' thinking around an agreed dilemma (Intrator et al. 1992). Having a protocol to follow can also feel containing at the start of a therapist's career by managing the choices available. However, protocols cannot provide guidance on the more ambiguous elements of decision-making, such as who defines the issue that the protocol aims to address (Lane and Corrie 2006). Moreover, protocols cannot provide guidance on how practitioners should innovate, redesign or even redefine choices as new information comes to light. Perhaps this is why there is some evidence to suggest that while manualized interventions may help novice practitioners, they can prove constraining and detrimental for effective and experienced therapists (Castonguay et al. 1996; Westen et al. 2004).

De Bono (1995) has examined how different types of situations call for different types of thinking skill through use of a hunting metaphor. Specifically, he describes our rational, analytical skills as akin to 'shooting'. Shooting questions refer to those we ask when we have a distinct target; we know what we are aiming for and have our outcome (a single, correct answer) clearly in sight. Here, accuracy is very important. Suppose, for example, that you have been working with a client for a while and from all the discussions you have had, and all the data you have collected, you have a specific hypothesis (target in sight) and you want to find out if it is accurate. In order to test this hypothesis, your questions become more and more specific until you receive confirmation that the hypothesis is correct (or incorrect). You have hit the target. We could see this type of thinking skill as being particularly beneficial when you want to turn a broad aim into a specific measurable, achievable, realistic, time-framed (SMART; Locke and Latham 1990) goal, when you are attempting to ascertain whether a client meets diagnostic criteria for a particular psychiatric problem, when accuracy of approach is essential or when you are working with a clearly defined and straightforward obstacle that lends itself well to simple problem-solving techniques.

Fishing questions, in contrast, are those which involve searching, exploring and uncovering. Like the act of fishing itself, knowledge and skill are exercised in the process of increasing the likelihood of a catch but the approach taken is essentially one of stepping back and waiting to see what takes the bait. In therapy practice, a 'fishing' approach will entail skilled listening, use of open and exploratory questions, searching for links as yet unarticulated, and remaining with the uncertainty until we are clear what our target is. It might also be akin to those occasions where we need to make use of metaphors or analogies to illustrate key ideas or create innovative interventions to help clients move forward. Here, the therapist is operating almost in the role of 'designer' where decisions have to be crafted and chosen from a range of possibilities.

If you are attempting to shoot when it would be preferable to fish, you are likely to miss a great deal and could undermine the therapy by forcing a client's story into an interpretive framework of your own choosing rather than being responsive to the client's needs. We would see this danger as being very prevalent in the current climate where therapists often feel that they face considerable pressure to 'get on with it', and demonstrate swift results and changes on symptom profiles.

What frameworks of reasoning do I need to make good decisions in therapy?

Shooting and fishing are metaphors for different mental operations – the one focused and directed, the other exploratory and open to what may emerge. But the ability to use both, as well as the ability to decide which to use and when, relies on a good degree of cognitive sophistication. Beyer (1985) has argued that we need to appreciate that effective thinking is both a frame of mind and a number of specific mental operations. This distinction is useful in that it enables us to consider how effective thinking is dependent upon at least two specific components: a specific set of mental operations or thinking skills and also an attitudinal outlook underpinned by a distinct framework of reasoning.

There is also a useful distinction in terms of different ways in which we come to know the world. Bruner (1987, 1990) identifies two primary modalities of cognitive functioning. The first concerns abstract knowledge and general concepts (paradigmatic) which enable us to make sense of and solve practical problems through a reliance on consistency, logic and rationality. The second is concerned with knowledge that is rich in context and idiosyncratic meaning (narrative). Narrative thought consists in telling stories about the self to self and others. We make sense of our experience through the act of story construction. Both are powerful and distinct forms of expression. The transmission of knowledge relies on each modality (Deslauriers 1992).

Within cognitive psychology, Teasdale and Barnard (1993) have differentiated *propositional* and *implicational* levels of meaning. The propositional refers to knowing what can be expressed linguistically and can be evaluated as true or false, while the implicational level refers to the more holistic type of knowing to which Bruner and others seem to allude.

Propositional statements might include the following examples:

- I am 6 feet 4 inches tall.
- Today is Friday.
- You are reading this book in India.
- This client meets diagnostic criteria for post-traumatic stress disorder.

These statements relate to different topics, but they share certain properties. They can be evaluated, in a relatively straightforward fashion, for their accuracy when measured against an external criterion. If you met us, you would be able to establish whether either of us is 6 feet 4 inches tall; you could confirm or disconfirm the day of the week, as indeed you could the location in which you are reading this book. The statement relating to diagnosis is no different in this regard; it can be established to be true or false (at least in principle) by examining client data against a table of criteria from a diagnostic manual. This is the quality of thinking that underpins much of the literature which has questioned the accuracy of practitioners' decision-making.

Now consider the following statements that represent the implicational level:

- My heart is broken.
- You light up my world.
- The wind blew right through me.
- His tone of voice was as cold as ice.

Here, the meaning conveyed is of a different order. The implicational level often seems to resonate more closely with what it means to be human and to our own unique experience. To attempt to treat the above as propositional statements ('Is it *really* the case that your heart is broken? If we took an X-ray of your heart right now would it show that your heart was *actually* broken?') would be to miss the point. The language of fiction, poetry and metaphor would be similar examples of where implicational meanings are conveyed. Through the implicational or narrative, important human concerns can be shared and addressed, but not in a way that relates directly to propositional language.

As our theories, models of therapy and evidence base have expanded, psychology and psychotherapy have acquired an enormous amount of information on how to work within the propositional or paradigmatic domain. However, there remains a lack of guidance on how best to work with the implicational or narrative domain. This is potentially highly problematic when we consider that narration is the principal way in which people make sense of their experience (Hillman 1983; McLeod 2000).

Exercise 9: *Working with fairy or folk tales as an example of the implicational domain*

It has been said that a key function of fairy tales or folk tales is to alert children to the ways of the world that they would not be able to grasp so easily if presented in a factual manner (Tatar 2003). We could see this as an example of the implicational domain. What do you think are the key messages in the following fairy stories? If these are not known to you, consider other folk tales from your childhood and ask the question again.

- Cinderella?
- Sleeping Beauty?
- Hansel and Gretel?
- Snow White and the Seven Dwarfs?
- The Frog Prince?

From levels of knowing to cognitive mindset: what mindset do you need in order to make good decisions in therapy?

Stice (1987) has proposed that there are a number of attitudes that, if adopted, are likely to improve our decision-making capability and enable us to develop the mental operations that underpin this. These, he suggests, are:

- an ability to cope with complexity, confusion and conflicting perspectives and to contain the discomfort to which this may give rise;
- a willingness to accept anomalies in the information available to us;
- courage to take appropriate risks;
- the desire to improve our problem-solving abilities.

Stice argues that creative people tend to have a positive mental attitude to problem-solving, approaching dilemmas and the decision-making to which they give rise as opportunities for new experiences and a vehicle for enriching their repertoire of thinking skills. The capacity to tolerate ambiguity and to cope with complexity has been considered by Owen and Lindley (2010), who highlight that a therapist can be skilled at differentiating counselling theories but not have the ability to engage in critical thinking. In their work on cognitive complexity, Owen and Lindley (2010) have argued that therapists need critical thinking skills that enable them to find ways of addressing clinical dilemmas that have no clear answers. Moreover, they ascertain that a goal of therapy training is to enhance students' capacity for reflection and critical thinking in such contexts. They propose that we need to be able to:

- identify and differentiate between relevant theoretical constructs (such as understanding the types of intervention used by psycho-dynamic and behavioural approaches);
- have an awareness of cognitive processes (such as being aware of, and able to reflect upon, our own cognitive processes when working with a client);
- reason about dilemmas that occur in the context of practice (i.e. think our way through real-world dilemmas that have no definitive answer and which require us to a take account of a range of factors, including the context in which any decision is made).

We would see the first point – differentiating theoretical constructs – as being a cognitive skill that can be usefully developed within formal therapy training and supervision. The second point – developing an awareness of one's own cognitive processes – can be usefully developed within supervision and through use of the exercises in this book. The final point – gaining experience of reasoning about dilemmas encountered in the real, and often messy, world of practice – relies on an amalgam of formal training, ongoing supervision, reflection, enhancing critical thinking skills and attending carefully to one's continuing professional development.

Exercise 10:   *Which thinking skills do you use?*

Spend some time reflecting on the reasoning frameworks and thinking skills you use on a daily basis. Select a day and use this as an opportunity to audit the decisions you make in key areas and the mental operations that underpin them. See if you can develop a sense of the range of skills you use – those based on accuracy (such as reversing a car into a parking space without hitting another vehicle; calculating the exact amount on a bill that you need to pay) and those based on other types of reasoning skill (such as making up a bedtime story). Try to categorize each according to the frameworks reviewed in this chapter.

- Which ones do you use the most?
- Which ones do you use the least?
- At this stage of your career, which ones might it be most useful to develop? How could you go about doing so?

Write down your observations and reflections in your learning log. Are there any reasoning styles or thinking skills discussed in this chapter with which you think it would be helpful to experiment?

Conclusion

In evaluating some of the strengths and limitations of the literature on therapists' decision-making, it is important to avoid seeing the debate in all-or-nothing terms (remember the cognitive distortions we looked at in Chapter 1!). We are certainly not dismissing the importance of accuracy, but rather proposing that the emphasis on determining accuracy has at times occurred at the expense of a fuller exploration of the types of thinking, decision-making and problem-solving skills that are needed in therapy practice. If this is true, then it is important to consider how framing the debate in this way will help and hinder therapists who wish to improve their decision-making skills. One obvious implication is that we do not, as yet, have sufficient information or guidelines on how therapists can systematically develop their skills at the narrative/implicational level.

Our decisions will be the product of many influences. Making successful decisions in therapy practice requires a range of cognitive operations that can be applied to a constantly changing stream of interpersonal exchanges. From this chapter, we can conclude that the kinds of decisions therapists are attempting to make in practice are not always consistent with the emphasis on accuracy, reliability and outcome that has been the focus of much of the literature to date. Perhaps this is why practitioners have relied more on personal experience than the decision-making literature, of which many do not seem to be aware (Turk and Salovey 1985). Eliminating error does not, it seems, automatically pave the way for developing better ideas (de Bono 1995). Providing a quality service to our clients relies on an ability to generate new possibilities, a capacity to tailor technical knowledge to the needs of the individual client, an ability to move seamlessly between propositional and implicational domains of knowing, and a willingness to think about how our decisions are always relative and context-dependent.

The critical task is knowing when to focus on thinking skills that will promote accuracy and when to focus on thinking skills that will enable a more innovative or creative approach. The former will be most useful when:

- the problem is uncontentious;
- the priority is to make a decision and take action;

- the aim is to achieve uniformity of decision and action to minimize risk to a client or protect against litigation;
- further exploration is likely to confuse rather than clarify.

The latter is most useful when you need to:

- gain a better understanding of how different stakeholders might have different ideas about the best way forward;
- find new ways of thinking about a particular dilemma;
- engineer new possibilities for action;
- engage curiosity, interest and hope.

(Lane and Corrie 2006).

This raises the critical question of the context in which you are working and, in particular, the extent to which this is an individual or a collective decision and how far you are working with known (propositional) or unknown (particularly implicational) parameters. In the next chapter, we explore this further by thinking about some of the decision-making skills that are required in states of uncertainty (the unknown). However, before we conclude this chapter, spend some time thinking about the scenario in Sarah's log, below. Based on the ideas discussed in this chapter, what do you think are the main styles of reasoning and mental operations that Sarah's supervisor used to help her reframe her response to a personally challenging situation?

Sarah's log

Early in my career as I was in the process of establishing myself as an author, I submitted an article for publication that was rejected. The feedback was very critical and deeply shook my faith in my ability to produce anything of a publishable standard.

My supervisor noticed that I seemed low and invited me to share with him what was troubling me. He listened carefully and then, apparently ignoring my current dilemma, told me the story of a famous rock band who had recorded an album that no one wanted to produce. The band took the album to one record producer after another, each time getting the same response – a rejection. Close to giving up, the band eventually agreed to try one last time. This time the response was positive and the album became what was then one of the best-selling albums of all time.

My supervisor offered no critical appraisal of my article, no reassuring words about the difficulty of getting work published, or encouragement to use the feedback constructively. He just told me this story.

A couple of weeks later, I asked him if he would look over my article and give me some feedback, which was constructive but critical. But somehow this time I could take the feedback without feeling as though I had failed. A while later, having rewritten the article, it was published by another journal.

Years later, this story about persistence in the face of setback remains one to which I return whenever I am faced with disappointment.

✍ Learning summary

One idea I have found useful in this chapter is. . .

. . . .

. . . .

One thing I would like to experiment with, having read this chapter, is. . .

. . . .

. . . .

Was there anything I didn't quite understand? (If so, I will find out more by. . .)

. . . .

. . . .

3 Going wider, going deeper: decision-making in states of uncertainty

> **In this chapter you will learn about:**
> - the steadily growing literature on decision-making in states of uncertainty
> - the types of narrative and implicational frameworks that are needed by practitioners
> - the implications of this literature for therapy practice when the need is to innovate
>
> **By reading this chapter you will be able to:**
> - evaluate the various approaches to innovative and creative thinking processes
> - use a range of narrative and implicational operations that are needed in practice
> - create your own approach to novel ways of problem-solving
> - include innovative and creative approaches in your decision-making

Introduction

In the previous chapters we examined the literature which has attempted to investigate the accuracy of practitioners' decision-making and clinical judgement. We then considered some of the debates surrounding this literature and made the case that while accuracy is an important aspect of knowing whether our decisions are sound, it is an insufficient basis for working effectively with our clients. To address this we identified the broader set of reasoning skills that practitioners need to help them navigate the day-to-day challenges of professional practice.

In this chapter we continue to examine the range of reasoning skills that therapists need to work effectively with clients. With particular reference to innovation and design, and drawing on implicational forms of knowing, we offer methods for helping you develop these skills in your own practice.

What happens when the structured decision-making models do not seem to fit?

The hope underpinning evidence-based practice is that it might provide blueprints for how to act in a given case. For example, if a client is depressed we apply the 'proven' best practice approach for dealing with depression in the form of an intervention that is empirically supported (for an introduction to evidence-based practice and the debates surrounding it, see Corrie 2010).

However, individuals often present with complexities that do not seem to fit simple diagnosis to treatment options. Moreover, when they do, unanticipated events can present themselves that require a response from the therapist. So let us look at some of the ways in which complexities might present, even from the first encounter.

David's log

As a therapist working in a hospital outpatient clinic receiving referrals from a primary care service, I received a letter from a general practitioner referring a 50-year-old married woman suffering from depression. The GP believed that she would benefit from a course of cognitive behavioural therapy. I collected the client from the waiting room and noticed that as soon as she saw me her face dropped. We reached the consulting room and sat down. I had a referral letter in front of me outlining her diagnosis and the GP's preferred treatment option, which matched our service offer. I also had sitting in front of me a client who already looked unhappy. I wondered where to begin.

Exercise 11: *Seeking to understand clients' expectations when they meet you*

Imagine that this is your client. Take a moment to think about this woman and both of you together in the consulting room for the first time. Based on your experience so far (including books and articles you have read and any teaching you have experienced, any work you may have done with clients or your own experience as a client in therapy), what would you see as some of the hopes, fears and expectations that might be present in the room? List them in your learning log.

Now consider your list. Whose hopes, fears and expectations did you consider? The client's? Your own? The GP's? The client's partner or significant others? A number of individuals are impacting on the encounter, including those of whom you might be unaware, such as children or colleagues. Would you mention to her what you noticed in the waiting room? Would you start with the referral letter? Would you start with what has brought her to the clinic?

Let us suppose you start with the referral letter. This immediately sets up a stance towards her that defines her as a depressed patient and creates the expectation that cognitive behaviour therapy is likely to be offered as a solution. As such, you might begin to explore how long she has been depressed, what it is like to be depressed, her thoughts, feelings and behaviours when depressed and the circumstances in which she is more or less depressed. You might explore her understanding of what cognitive behavioural therapy involves and her willingness to engage with this approach. She seems to be a willing person who believes the doctor knows best and is, therefore, prepared to agree to your plan. Do you now continue and ignore that look in the waiting room, or raise it – or believe that if it is important to her she will raise it? What would you do next?

If this chapter was offering a structured decision process we would probably now offer you a next step. Instead, we will leave you with your tension because the key point in this chapter is that the tension is a source of creativity. Rather than seeking to remove it, we would like to encourage you to embrace it. We will talk more about this later in the chapter.

The need to embrace ambiguity

One of the central features of the therapy literature has been the debate on the role of the client's story and that of the diagnosis given. As the above example illustrates, there is a tension that emerges from having to decide whether you are we dealing with a depressed client or a client with a story to tell.

Decisions of this kind are not solely about the client in front of you, but also about the way in which your service defines itself. They also reflect your own preferences and tolerance for ambiguity. In a study of decision-making across a wide range of organizations, Rajan et al. (2000) point to the preferences that exist for how we conduct our work roles. Some like structured systems, quality manuals and a clear plan they can enact. Others prefer to have a clear goal but the freedom to explore how best to achieve it. A third group, while retaining a sense of the overall mission, will seek to refine the task and find new ways to serve their clients. Similarly, in therapy some may prefer a framework of evidence-based practice, or a manual or protocol which provides guidelines on what to do and what to expect. For others the story is the starting point of an exploration into unknown territory. The latter requires a willingness to be comfortable with ambiguity and to be prepared to work with the issues that emerge.

Some have argued that ambiguity is central to all our work. As Strasser and Strasser (1997: 15) observe: 'If we accept that from the moment we are born we are faced with inescapable uncertainties and inherent limitations, then it also becomes apparent that we all strive in our own way to form and create a framework or structure upon which we hope to depend'. This is equally so for therapists and clients. The question for the therapist is how much of the client's framework they need to comprehend to be helpful and how much are they prepared to depart from their own understanding to deliver on that offer.

As we seek to formulate an understanding of our clients' needs, the generic models we are taught may not always seem to fit. The stories our clients tell contain elements that fit predetermined categories but then wander into areas we could not have predicted. We learn, therefore, how to assist our clients to formulate the accounts they present into narratives that are meaningful to them, us and other stakeholders. However, we do this in a broader context which includes local service requirements, national guidelines and global influences on how health care should be provided. These enable and constrain what is considered to be acceptable practice (Corrie and Lane 2010). The requirements that these influences dictate may not fit the story the client is trying to tell. Thus we are faced with a dilemma: do we work with the client's story as they want to tell it or do we require the client to tell a story in a way that fits the provision available? Decisions we need to make that stem from this dilemma include the following:

- Do we work from features common for a condition or features that distinguish the individual client (the diagnostic or individual narrative dilemma)?
- Do we examine parts in sequence rather than the whole (the theory versus the person dilemma)?

- Do we see each aspect of the client's behaviour as an outcome of specific causes or as an expression of that person's overall position in the world (the relatedness dilemma)?

Working in different professional spaces

Whatever it is we are deciding, the issue at hand will be a decision made in a context whose features influence how we act. Two such features seem particularly relevant to the decision-making process:

1. What is the level of agreement about what we should do?
2. How well can we predict the outcome of what we decide to do?

For some of our clients, we can arrive at clear agreements on the areas to be addressed. The problem can be clearly and uncontentiously defined; all parties involved are prepared to work within those parameters and there is a good evidence base to inform decisions about what is likely to be effective. At the other extreme we have no agreement and no likelihood of being able to predict the outcome. The situation appears and feels chaotic. In between there is the space sometimes called the 'edge of chaos' (Pascale et al. 2000) in which we can find creative solutions (which may not resemble the descriptions in the literature) if we are prepared to work with the tensions to which the situation gives rise.

Using the two questions above, derived from the work of complexity theorist, Ralph Stacey (2002) and adapting the work of Corrie and Lane (2010), Cavanagh and Lane (2012) have been presenting the idea of 'different spaces' within which different types of decision and ways of working become viable. These are very relevant to the types of dilemmas we encounter therapy. See which ones are familiar to you.

The rational space

The rational space assumes a high level of agreement about what to do, a high chance that any agreed action can be carried out effectively and that the outcome will be as predicted. It is the space within which empirically led approaches can work. Decisions can be made using an existing protocol, evidence base or hypothesis-testing framework because the rational space:

- assumes a cause-effect and linear process;
- works from the client's story but views the story as a unique example of a more general stock of stories which can be informed by an evidence base;

- overlaps with paradigmatic or propositional forms of knowing that are abstract, logical and predictable.

(See Chapter 6, 'Sarah's log: Treating Richard's panic disorder', for an example of this.)

The emergent space

This assumes some level of disagreement about what to do and only moderate likelihood of being able to determine outcomes. It is the space in which the ideas have to emerge from the engagement between therapist and client and where the tensions have to be embraced and used as sources of creativity. It is where the story will emerge from the process of working rather than being framed within an existing evidence base from the outset. Emergent stories work 'from the ground up' (i.e. from the client's story rather than from a predefined notion of what might help). In the emergent space:

- we look for themes that emerge in the conversation;
- we use tension and anxiety creatively rather than see emotions as something to be controlled;
- we are able to operate with ambiguity.

(See Chapter 1, 'Case study: How to help Emily with her low self-esteem', for an example of this.)

The chaotic space

This assumes we have little or no agreement about what to do, and even if we do choose to act we cannot predict the outcome. It is an unnerving space for many of us, as therapists and as clients. It is a space where the temptation is to cling to any theory or technique that offers some hope and relief from the tension inherent in not knowing. Even among theorists working in this field, there is widespread disagreement about how chaotic situations should be managed. There are those who believe that the leader has to provide a clear vision of the way forward in order to reduce anxiety (Snowden and Boone 2007). Others (Cavanagh and Lane 2012) believe that the anxiety has to be contained but not reduced, as it creates the opportunity to generate new stories. There is agreement, nevertheless, that whatever approach leaders take, they have to create a safe structure to enable others to work. The structure:

- provides boundaries using predetermined lenses to enable new stories;

- helps hold anxiety so that we can work with the context;
- is most appropriate in chaotic contexts.

(See Chapter 5, 'David's log: Example of mission within the individual unknown quadrant', for an example of this.)

Approaches to decision-making for different professional spaces

In Chapters 1 and 2 we looked at the first of these spaces where structured decision-making models seemed to make sense. In trying to find ways to work in the other two spaces (emergent and chaotic) we cannot offer neat, structured decision-making tools. Unfortunately, these spaces do not lend themselves to these types of methods. Indeed, given that an inherent feature of chaos is that we move in and out of order, we cannot predict outcomes and, therefore, cannot know which decision process will work. Rather we seek to find ways to keep the tension in play and allow for creative solutions to emerge.

If we think of these spaces as being in constant flux, some approaches emerge as potentially useful decision-making aids. Next, we look at four possibilities which can help us as we move through different professional spaces. These are:

- taking a different perspective;
- taking a wider perspective;
- taking a deeper perspective;
- taking a more complex perspective.

We will suggest ways to do each of these as we proceed.

Taking a different perspective

There are many who have looked at the question of helping people take a different perspective. Inherent in most of them is encouraging the willingness to experiment with ideas so that new possibilities can be formed. One of the earliest and still most useful distinctions is that drawn by de Bono between shooting and fishing questions. The former have a clear target in view but the latter explore around a topic (see Chapter 2 for a more detailed description). His work on lateral thinking (de Bono 1985, 2006) provides a way to examine this. A particularly helpful tool to use with clients is to encourage them to put on different thinking hats so that they can take a different perspective. In research conducted in many contexts he shows how this enables decision-making where people might otherwise get stuck. Try this for yourself.

Exercise 12: *Using the six thinking hats to take a different perspective*

Think about something that is currently troubling you and where you are feeling unable to decide how to move forward. Describe the issue briefly in your learning log.
Now using each of the six hats (in any order) explore the issue again.

- White hat: focus on information gathering
  - What is the issue, where do you want to be, what do you need to know to get there?
- Red hat: focus on feelings, intuition
  - What feels the best way forward? What seems to be appropriate?
- Black hat: focus on caution and critical thinking
  - What might get in the way, what can you do about it?
- Yellow hat: focus on benefits, values and ways forward
  - What will be different when you get there?
- Green hat: focus on creativity, possibilities
  - What possibilities might you have or create?
- Blue hat: focus on organizing thinking – what to focus on, the plan of action, etc.
  - What tasks and actions are needed, who will do what, when?

What options for action now occur to you? Is your perspective on what might be possible any different from before?

Another way to change perspective is to switch focus from the problem to the solution. Thus, we become solution-focused rather than problem-focused (we have changed the perspective). The assumptions here are the following:

- Even persistent problems are not present all the time.
- If you know where you are headed it is easy to get there.
- Look for exceptions.
- Do more of what works.
- Do less of what does not work.
- Ask yourself: 'If things were different how would they look?'

Central to this process is creating a space in which the possibility of a different perspective can emerge.

One author who has focused on the nature of that space and how to create it is Nancy Kline (2003, 2005). Kline is concerned with how we create space in which thinking can emerge. The crucial point for our approach here is to identify and replace limiting assumptions with a more powerful worldview. The aim is to look at and replace one limiting assumption at a time, relevant to the presenting issue. There is a six-stage process as follows:

1. Exploration (what do you want to think about?).
2. Further goal (what would you like to accomplish in the rest of this session?).
3. Assumptions (what are you assuming that is stopping you from accomplishing your goal?):
   (a) What is the key assumption?
   (b) Is that assumption true?
   (c) What are your reasons for thinking that?
       (i) Transition question – what are you assuming that holds you back?
       (ii) Invitation question – what could you assume that would help you achieve your goal?
4. Incisive question (if you knew that that assumption, in (ii) above, was true, how would you accomplish your goal?).
5. Recording (the client takes responsibility for recording the question and the action to be taken).
6. Appreciation (the client and therapist identify a quality they respect in each other).

In the space created between client and therapist the aim is to ask questions that provide the time to think and, therefore, facilitate new possibilities. The limiting assumptions that hold us back from taking a new perspective can be dismantled. (Note that this is a summary only. For a more detailed review, see Kline 2003.)

Taking a wider perspective

One way in which our past patterns can hamper therapy is if our theoretical view of the world is limited to seeing behaviour purely as the outcome of a limited range of factors, such as the result of internal processes, maladaptive thinking or past role models. Sometimes it is important to take a wider perspective that enables us to focus on a very different context. A number of theorists have looked at the wider context impacting on us and the way we make use of our experience to learn. Key among these are Wilber (2000) and Kolb (1984). Chapman (2010) has integrated these models to look at the wider perspectives we might employ, and this is reflected in the sections that follow. Wilber's (2000) model provides a meta-framework for integrated growth and development. He argues that we have to pay attention to both individual and collective factors operating at an interior or exterior level. Kolb's (1984) model provides a way of looking at how we respond to and transform our experience. An individual will generally experience something concrete in the context of the collective; that is, something happens to them 'out there'. To make sense of that experience the individual needs to make use of the intension dimension, move inwards, and reflect on the experience. Having reflected on it, the person starts to develop some theory or concept about the experience. Abstract conceptualization, however, is not something that belongs purely to the individual; it is influenced by the culture or system in which the individual finds him- or herself. Kolb (1984) conceptualizes experiential learning as a developmental process that is the product of both personal and social knowledge. The individual's state of development flows from the transaction of the individual's personal experience and the particular system of social knowledge with which they interact.

Having developed a theory, the individual then needs to engage the extension dimension and actively experiment within the collective environment. The value of Kolb's (1984) model is that it is context- and content-independent. Let us try an exercise based on this approach.

Exercise 13: *Using Chapman's integration to take a wider perspective*

Take a moment to think about a decision-making dilemma that has caused you difficulty. Briefly describe the issue in your learning log. Now explore the concern using one aspect from each of Wilber's four categories.

Individual/Interior	**Individual/Exterior**
Thoughts/ambitions	Neuro-muscular system
Feelings	Genetics
Mood	Body sensations
Sensory input	Behaviour
Images	Actions

Collective/Interior	Collective/Exterior
Language	Natural/human systems
Social world	Technology
Rituals/history	Processes and structures
Customs	Physical laws
Culture – organization/family	Objects

Start by describing the actual, concrete example that is causing you difficulty. Then consider, in turn, one item from each of the four categories. For example, think about the image that this dilemma conjures up. Then take some time to recollect the bodily sensations that this generates. Now consider the customs governing the way decisions are made in this context that are preventing resolution of the dilemma. Finally, identify the processes and structures in operation in your context which are constraining making this decision.

Having looked at the concrete example and reflected upon it in each of the four categories, what possibilities now occur to you? If you add other elements, what occurs? How is your perspective wider than before? How might you now see the world differently and create a way forward? By acting on this you will create a new concrete experience and thus complete a learning cycle.

Taking a deeper perspective

The work of Kolb, Wilber and Chapman discussed in the previous section opens up the possibility of a broader range of perspectives but also different ways of grasping and responding to our experience. One group of authors who have particularly focused on different ways of grasping experience include those exploring how we can sense our experience differently (Gendlin 1997; Senge et al. 2005). These authors invite us to go deeper and work from felt knowledge, not just rational decision-making at the propositional level, as discussed in Chapter 2.

Within counselling there is a tradition, established in the 1960s in the human potential movement, for exploration of what Gendlin (1997) calls the philosophy of the implicit. Gendlin (1996) was interested in why some psychotherapy clients improved while others did not. He argued that what made the difference was the client's internal process. Those who were more successful were checking inside themselves for an embodied sense of their situation. Gendlin developed an approach to help clients find their own intricate bodily sensed experience. This level of awareness he called the *felt sense*.

The felt sense is holistic in nature and as we come to be aware at this level we can begin to feel some release of tension. It is this that tells us we have made contact with a deeper level of awareness within ourselves. This comes not through the action of the therapist but through the felt experience of the client. Resolution comes in small, successive steps involving contacting the felt sense and waiting for something new to emerge.

Out of this work a number of tools have been developed to approach problem-solving at the level of the implicit or implicational. One of the critiques of our models of psychotherapy is that they represent the constructions of therapists, for therapists, that can all too easily be imposed on clients in ways that are experienced as unhelpful or undermining (Davison 1991; cited in Davison and Gann 1998). Contacting your 'felt sense' response to what is occurring provides a potential counter-balance to this through encouraging you and the client to establish resonance with the proposed way forward. These tools are readily available (see Gendlin 1997).

Senge et al. (2005) have also critiqued structured decision models. They see them as adequate only if the past is a good guide to the future. In contrast, the ability to recognize new forces shaping change requires a sensing of influencers before they emerge. This way of arriving at a decision point is fundamentally different from exercising a rational analysis of options in order to arrive at a considered outcome. It involves much deeper levels of feeling and being (according to Senge) and involves becoming highly attuned to our sensory experience. Here, the need is to suspend our rational thinking to redirect our attention to the living processes within us. It requires us to be totally present to ourselves and in the space around us and to be alive to what is emerging from within us. This leads to the capacity to sense something new and act in accordance with the felt knowledge generated.

Exercise 14: *Working with presence*

Working with between one and four others, take some time to consider those moments when you have felt most fully engaged – when every fibre of your being has felt awake and alert. As each person spends time exploring this, and telling their story, avoid any tendency to try to analyse or explain the experience (stay out of the rational!). As you listen, listen intentionally to try to connect to your sense of that moment (the felt sense). Each person takes turns. Once you have all listened and connected, explore any shared sense. What is held in common?

The features that make this type of conversation more productive are when there is a desire to build common intent, listen to others and respond to what life calls you to do (co-initiating). You also need to observe closely, go to the places where you see the most potential and listen with your heart and an open mind (co-sensing). You need to connect to sources of inspiration, stay with a place of silence and allow inner knowing to emerge (pre-sensing). Test out the inner knowing that has emerged in living examples (co-creating). Finally, embody the new in ways that facilitate seeing and acting within entire ecosystems (co-evolving). Senge et al. (2005) provide a detailed account of this process.

Taking a more complex perspective

The idea of uncertainly being an irreducible state (i.e. not something we can reduce to component parts in order to take a step-by-step approach) has a long history in many fields. From Keynes in economics, existential models in philosophy and Buddhism, to modern theories in complexity sciences, decision-making under conditions of uncertainly has attracted attention (Lane et al. 2009).

When faced with complex states we are confronted by situations in which cause and effect are distant in time and space. We either do not know, or cannot know, what causes events to happen. In making a decision we are not, therefore, seeking new facts in order to arrive at a rational and linear solution based on the notion that 'x causes y'. Search as we might for such equations, we will not find them. The reason is that in complex situations the dependency of each event on others is unknowable. We have to move away from probabilities towards possibilities.

This is particularly true in organizational contexts. As the sociologist Merton (1938), and more recently Livingston (1997), have identified, within any organization there will be many cultures operating, some which are dominant (manifest) and some which are hidden (latent). The manifest is the official version, which lays out the organization's purpose, the perspectives it employs to understand its world and the procedures that are used to make things happen. However, there are also in operation any number of latent cultures involving groups of people who hold different purposes and perspectives and, therefore, operate alternative processes for making decisions. The basis on which action happens may not, therefore, be as the manifest culture would state.

The key to decision-making in complex spaces is to ensure conditions that enable the latent to emerge. According to Cavanagh and Lane (2012), eight factors facilitate this:

1. The quality of the conversations determines the quality of the organization.
2. Anxiety needs to be managed, not removed.

3. Build trust or spend considerable amounts of time managing unnecessary anxiety.
4. Celebrate diversity, as it is the source of creativity.
5. Do not try to control the system as this is not possible. However:
6. You still have to act!
7. Quality of action is not judged by outcome. An action is good because:
   - it fits with the demands of the environment;
   - it is fundamentally moral and ethical in nature.
8. Strategy itself is emergent – it is an ongoing, iterative, conversation.

Let us try an exercise using these ideas.

Exercise 15: *Approaching tensions in complex spaces*

As we have seen, turbulence creates inevitable dilemmas concerning the level of agreement about our purpose and what we do, the predictability of outcomes and the central role played by the stories we tell about ourselves and each other.

Rational language, grounded in propositional statements, can have a dominating effect, creating the illusion of certainty and control, influencing people's assumptions and actions and blocking exploration of alternative and different perspectives. How, then, do we turn towards the tension rather than seek to control it?

One useful tool is that of dialogue. In dialogue we seek to approach the tension and explore it rather than reduce it or resolve it through debate. In debate the different parties present their arguments, try to defend their position and prove the other party wrong (the 'you lose, I win' scenario). In discussion the same might happen, but, at its most productive, each party seeks to find a common ground or possibly a compromise (the 'we both win' scenario). However, in dialogue you suspend your own position and become curious about the other's position. You seek to understand together how you each see the issue. As you seek to understand that position tension will arise, but you sit with the tension rather than try to eradicate it; the tension is seen as a path to a more creative position. You then try to decide together what might be a way forward. This often takes the form of a generative dialogue in which you either adopt a bigger perspective which incorporates both positions but expands them, or reach a new position that you could not have arrived at individually.

So when working with someone where you have a disagreement try using a dialogue process to see whether you can arrive at a bigger perspective, or a new position.

Conclusion

In this chapter we have sought to explore decision-making in areas where a structured process has less value. In particular, we have been interested in decision-making under conditions of uncertainty where it is not possible to decide on a best course of action since factors of influence are non-linear. To help us manage these more complex decision-making scenarios, we have suggested thinking about your practice as taking place in one of three professional spaces (the rational, emergent or chaotic). We have also suggested that although structured linear decision-making processes are not suitable for the complex, emergent and chaotic spaces, there are still steps you can take to improve the quality of your decisions in these types of environment (namely, taking a different, wider, deeper or more complex perspective).

If you are at the very start of your career, we hope that you will have an opportunity to consolidate your core therapeutic competencies and develop your confidence in rational space before being plunged into working with more complex needs in more chaotic settings. However, we also recognize that many practitioners are finding themselves faced with high levels of complexity at increasingly early stages of their working lives. For this reason, we wanted to ensure that you have at least some tools and strategies available to you, should you need them.

We started this chapter by suggesting that at the end of it, you would be able to evaluate some of the approaches to innovative and creative thinking processes that are now emerging, and use a range of narrative and implicational operations to support your practice. Having been introduced to these processes, we suggest that you create your own novel ways to solve problems and invite you to continue with this process in the weeks and months ahead.

The final task of this chapter to is to take the time to explore how you might develop a broader range of decision-making processes. Think about the different spaces we have explored. Which resonate with you in terms of your work context? Consider the types of decision models you currently use which fit well and which do not in those spaces. Are there gaps in the tools available to you? Might you need to think differently, more widely, deeper or in a more complex way?

Holding your answers in mind will prepare you well for the following chapters where we provide a framework for building your own approach to decision-making and explore further specific examples of decision-making contexts.

Learning summary

One idea I have found useful in this chapter is. . .

. . . .

. . . .

One thing I would like to experiment with, having read this chapter, is. . .

. . . .

. . . .

Was there anything I didn't quite understand? (If so, I will find out more by. . .)

. . . .

. . . .

Part II

How do we frame our decision-making in practice?

Having introduced you to the skills and styles of reasoning involved in successful decision-making, we now turn our attention to developing a framework that can help you develop a systematic approach. In Chapters 4–7 we present and elaborate upon a model called 'MAP' (an acronym for 'Mission–Attitude–Process') which you can use to inform your decision-making with clients at each stage of the therapeutic process. In Chapter 4 we provide a brief introduction to MAP, and then in Chapters 5–7 offer a more detailed analysis of each component. By examining each aspect in detail, we help you consider the different types of decisions and choices that are particularly relevant at each stage of therapy.

A key part of the way we approach MAP is to ensure that you can fully utilize knowledge which is personal to you as well as that which is embedded in collective processes and procedures. It will become your creation – one that enables you to justify the decisions you make as well as open them up to exploration and change.

4 MAP: a framework for decision-making in practice

In this chapter you will learn about:

- MAP, a framework that can guide your decision-making with clients
- the different components of MAP
- the context for applying your MAP

By reading this chapter you will be able to:

- begin to reflect on the relevance of MAP to your own learning, practice and development as a therapist
- use MAP to begin analysing what you bring to decision-making situations with your clients
- begin to think about the contexts in which you will need to develop your MAP

Introduction

In this chapter, we present a framework that you can use to guide your decision-making with clients at each stage of the therapeutic process. We briefly describe the framework and explain how it can be used to address a range of professional practice dilemmas. In Chapters 5–7 we will examine each of the components of the framework in greater detail, so you can see how it might relate to your practice.

Introducing MAP: a framework to guide your decision-making with clients

MAP (an acronym for 'Mission–Attitude–Process') is an atheoretical framework adapted from original work by Lane and colleagues (for an overview, see Lane and Corrie 2006). It has been investigated extensively, shown to be effective across a range of professional practice settings, and recently been developed for the purposes of self-coaching (see Corrie 2009). It has also been proposed as a useful framework for developing robust formulations of clients' needs (Corrie and Lane 2010).

The different components of MAP are as follows:

Mission

Before undertaking therapy with a client, it is vital to be clear about its fundamental purpose, or Mission. The shape that the therapy takes and the way the therapist reflects upon and evaluates their work will follow logically from there. Critical questions at this stage include the following:

- What is the purpose in working with the client?
- What are the main problems or concerns we need to explore?
- Who else is/needs to be involved and what are their expectations?
- What is the wider context that will influence how I work with this client?

Being clear about the Mission that underpins your work with clients supports you in making decisions relating to the early phases of therapy. It is concerned with the decisions that frame initial contact and whether or not work with a client proceeds beyond a referral letter or the initial consultation. Key decisions associated with this phase of the enquiry include:

- whether or not to work with a client;
- what information will be relevant to understanding the client's needs and how to go about gathering this information (i.e. developing an assessment strategy);
- how to establish a contract with a client;
- whether or not any ethical or legal issues are likely to arise;
- who else is involved in the client's life and/or care and may need to be informed.

In Part 1, we made the case that everyone involved in providing psychological interventions does so in an increasingly complex professional climate. By paying attention to the Mission component of MAP, we can better understand the impact of the many contexts in which therapists offer their services to clients, including the social, political and economic factors that are shaping our decisions about the services we provide (explicitly and implicitly) and to whom. Even where practitioners regard themselves as being able to operate relatively independently of these influences (e.g. when working in private practice), the contexts in which they are immersed still exert a level of influence that shapes their decision-making and choices in subtle ways.

Chapter 5 explains more about why it is essential for you to understand your professional context in order to develop a successful decision-making approach.

Attitude

The Attitude component of MAP is concerned with trying to understand those factors that influence the expectations of therapist and client, and that inform how the therapy unfolds. This includes beliefs about the nature and 'causes' of clients' difficulties, beliefs about the potential for change and ideas about what constitutes 'effective' practice. We will be aware of some of these factors, such as our beliefs about how therapy can assist change. However, as we saw in Chapter 2, some may represent foundational assumptions which have been absorbed through more indirect means and which may, therefore, be less available to introspection. Attitude includes our technical and psychological preparation for the role of therapist.

Awareness of the perspectives that you bring to your work can enable you to better appreciate the influence of beliefs that enhance and constrain your decision-making. It can also support you with planning a therapeutic intervention or strategy. Key decisions associated with this phase of the enquiry include:

- how to make sense of a client's concerns (what might be termed a formulation or case conceptualization, where theoretical knowledge is drawn upon to help make sense of the dilemmas the client is facing);
- planning an intervention strategy (where it makes sense to begin working together given the formulation);
- anticipating and/or managing any ethical or legal issues arising;
- communicating with other parties involved in the client's life and/or care.

Chapter 6 explains more about why it is essential for you to understand the perspectives that drive your work and how such awareness can enhance decision-making capability with clients.

Process

The Process component of MAP is concerned with the procedures, methods, tools and techniques needed to achieve the contract agreed with the client.

Once the Mission and Attitude have been defined, it is possible to structure a Process for the therapy and to select those methods that are necessary to achieve the desired outcome. Without Mission and Attitude clearly defined, the Process runs the risk of being a random selection of techniques from an ever-growing smorgasbord. Key decisions associated with designing a Process include:

- how to implement an action plan;
- how to identify suitable intervention strategies at each stage;
- how to evaluate progress – both in terms of whether the intervention plan is delivering the intended results and in terms of changes in the client's well-being;
- how to manage any ethical dilemmas, including risk, that arise during the course of therapy;
- how to know when to end therapy;
- how to evaluate the outcome of therapy.

Chapter 7 examines in greater detail why you need to be clear about the Process that informs your interactions with clients as you implement a particular therapeutic approach or method.

The context for our work: using MAP in practice

MAP has been derived from a framework used to define professional practice, namely Purpose, Perspective and Process (Lane and Corrie 2006). It was adapted to provide an enabling structure for individual decision-making (Corrie 2009) and thus we have used it here to structure this debate on decision-making in counselling and psychotherapy.

In the chapters that follow we guide you through the task of creating your Mission, defining the Attitude to inform it and devising a Process for working. However, we also recognize that the contexts in which we work are many and varied. As discussed in Chapter 3, they can be simple, complicated, complex or chaotic and the decision-making tools suitable for one context are not necessarily transferable to another. For example, we cannot select a tool built on the assumption that there is a simple, sequential explanation (the 'A leads to B leads to C' formula) when the situation faced is neither simple nor sequential. So in order to take account of this, we introduce the additional metaphor of 'quadrants' to encompass the range of contexts in which we, as therapists, might need to make decisions.

We start with the dimension from that which is known (or could, using existing tools, be discovered) to the opposite end where we are dealing with that which is unknown or possibly unknowable. This addresses the world of complexity within which professional practice is located. The other dimension we address is ways of seeing the world predicated on an individual view (our own and the client's) towards that derived from a collective understanding (which might exist in publicly/nationally defined service contexts).

Using this metaphor to think about structuring your MAP will, we hope, enable decision-making in whatever context you practice. Enjoy this part of the journey, as it is your MAP that you will be drawing.

✍ Learning summary

One idea I have found useful in this chapter is. . .

....

....

One thing I would like to experiment with, having read this chapter, is. . .

....

....

Was there anything I didn't quite understand? (If so, I will find out more by. . .)

....

....

5 Defining your Mission

In this chapter you will learn about:

- the importance of defining your Mission as a practitioner
- the relationship between individual and collective knowledge
- managing known, unknown and possibly unknowable knowledge

By reading this chapter you will be able to:

- reflect on the relevance of a coherent Mission to your own learning, practice and development as a therapist
- define your own Mission, and structure what you bring to decision-making situations with your clients

Introduction

As described in the previous chapter, before undertaking therapy with a client it is vital to be clear about its fundamental purpose, or Mission. The shape that the therapy takes and the way the therapist reflects upon and evaluates their work will follow logically from there. Critical questions associated with this phase of therapy include the following:

- What is the purpose in working with the client, mine and theirs?
- What are the main problems or concerns we need to explore?
- Who else is/needs to be involved and what are their expectations?
- What is the wider context that will influence how I work with this client?

A Mission may be defined as an overall purpose governing professional practice (such as how a professional body defines the core values, functions and activities of a counsellor or psychotherapist), how an individual therapist defines their role (including in relation to specific clients in a particular setting) or how a service defines its purpose (the nature of the service it provides, to whom, and what it sets out to achieve).

In this chapter, we examine why it is essential to have a secure sense of your Mission before undertaking therapy and to consider ways through which you might develop a more systematic and successful decision-making approach in relation to this.

Towards defining your Mission: which decision quadrant are you in?

When it comes to defining the Mission that will underpin the work which follows, there are two fundamental dimensions of which we need to take account:

1. Is the knowledge base on which we will rely known, unknown or maybe even unknowable?
2. Is that knowledge base individual (i.e. personal to us or the client) or is it part of a collective understanding (e.g. national guidelines on treatment for depression).

The Mission of the service in which you find yourself will vary as a function of these dimensions. This presents us with four possible quadrants through which we can define our Mission, as illustrated in Figure 1.

Each of these decision quadrants gives rise to a very different Mission and will require different approaches to decision-making. Of course it is possible to move between the different quadrants over time or even seek a synthesis, but what follows is an example of how each might look in the context of a specific setting in which therapy services are delivered.

Example of working in Quadrant 1: individual and known.

An individual counselling service within a school

In such a setting, students from the school can self-refer. The counsellor does not know what dilemmas the students will bring and, while offering confidentiality, does so within strict guidelines related to child protection regulations. The context for providing the service is clearly identified, and what can and cannot be offered is also defined. The counsellor may have a preferred theoretical orientation (say, a generic humanistic frame) but is open to other approaches if they make sense for the student. Hence, the counsellor does not know what problems they will encounter but does have methods of exploration to work with the client, drawn from existing models of practice, and a clear understanding of when to refer elsewhere. The counsellor is able to test out ideas, ask students to undertake tasks outside the sessions as experiments in behaviour, and can also, with

Quadrant 1. Individual and known	Quadrant 2. Collective and known
We are seekers after an individual truth to decide what will work for this client in this context. We can define goals for our work together based on individual case formulation using existing hypothesis-testing models; that is, we know how to seek the 'truth' but we do not know what that truth may look like until we have undertaken our analysis with the client. We are concerned with the accuracy and relevance of our decisions.	We can draw upon a collective understanding of the client's issues; we have an evidence base to help us structure our decisions that informs our decisions about what works best for clients presenting with this type of difficulty. We are seekers after that collective evidence and we try to match the client's goals to the evidence base. We are concerned with the congruence of our intervention with the collective guidelines for the issues we face.

Quadrant 4. Individual and unknown	Quadrant 3. Collective and unknown
We are faced with an individual journey into the unknown; neither client nor therapist knows what might be appropriate, how to generate change or if change is needed. Here we are seekers after truthfulness; that is, a sense of meaning in the context that we can hold with integrity, or a personal truth rather than a truth tested by experimentation in the world.	We are faced with a collective need or competing needs in a social system with no agreed understanding or knowledge base on which to draw; we cannot agree what to do for the best. In such a context we become seekers of a shared understanding that we can agree to use as a framework for decision-making in the absence of collective knowledge that could guide us.

Figure 1 Which decision quadrant are you In?

permission, seek information from relevant others (teachers, etc.). Goals can be collaboratively developed and are not defined externally to the therapeutic relationship. In this context, counsellor and client can be seekers of 'truth' (as it relates to the individual client) and much of the work will involve propositional knowledge whereby ideas can be tested and accepted or rejected for their accuracy and relevance. Hence, in terms of creating a Mission for the service, the counsellor will know:

- whether or not to work with a client: the limits are preset;
- what information will be relevant to understanding the client's needs and how to go about gathering this information (i.e. developing an assessment strategy);
- the basis for the contract with a client (which is negotiated within agreed parameters, such as child protection policies);

- the procedures and policies to follow should ethical or legal issues arise;
- who else is involved in the client's life and/or care, and may need to be informed.

Consider this type of service setting. If you were this counsellor working in this context, how would you define your Mission?

Example of working in Quadrant 2: collective and known.

A therapist working in a primary care service that is part of the 'Improving Access to Psychological Therapies' initiative. The service is based in a local community and receives referrals primarily from local general practitioners

When operating in this quadrant, there is a well-developed understanding between the service and referring agencies covering the type of issues addressed and the models used to assist clients. There are clear referral boundaries, and clients who do not fit these criteria are not accepted. There are established guidelines or even manuals setting out what will happen at different stages (including criteria for when to 'step up' clients into more intensive interventions), the possible timeframes for interventions and the methods that will be used. The service is evidence-based and the evidence relied upon has been publicly defined through national guidelines. It is thus drawn from a collective understanding between all stakeholders. The decision structures are publicly available, understood by all those involved, and only clients who can be incorporated into those structures are offered a service. There is a heavy emphasis on convergent thinking (i.e. where the aim is to achieve consensus on the issue and the best way forward). Goals are matched with the evidence base and coherence is sought between the service mission and the clients helped. The goals of the service have been collectively defined externally to the individual client. Like quadrant 1, the knowledge will be largely propositional. However, these propositions have been pre-tested and the role is essentially to validate that knowledge. Hence, in terms of creating a Mission for the service, therapists will be clear about the following:

- The clients likely to be referred. There is filtering of referrals to ensure a fit.
- Information relevant to understanding the client's needs is defined externally and incorporated into the operating procedures. There is a predefined assessment strategy rather than an approach developed between client and therapist.
- The contract with a client is largely or entirely standardized.

- If any ethical or legal issues are likely to arise, there is a process for addressing them.
- Who else is involved in the client's life and/or care, and may need to be informed, including reporting procedures to referring stakeholders.

Consider this type of service setting. If you were this counsellor working in this context, how would you define your Mission?

Example of working in Quadrant 3: collective and unknown.

A therapist working in community projects to support local groups in crisis situations

In this quadrant, some of the work may be very routine but some may involve highly complex issues, with multiple stakeholders taking contrasting views on the nature of the concern and the best way forward. It is not possible to know in advance which case will be routine and which will be complex. The counsellor may be faced with the task of having to manage dogmatic stances and conflicting power bases as well as unequal access to information and resources among those involved. In this quadrant, although counsellors may have general models for conflict resolution available to them, they will face the possibility of not knowing what to do or even if they should act at all. Whatever action they take will be highly unpredictable in its outcome and the effects of any intervention have the potential to harm as well as help. In this context, it will be not be possible to define goals that are acceptable to all parties. In some situations it will be possible to draw on an evidence base and tools for resolution, but these will not always fit. Therapists are likely to have to innovate and be highly creative in finding collective resolutions.

In this quadrant, the Mission is one of seeking a shared account, understanding, or narrative, constructed by the parties involved. Decision-making will have to be reflective and generative rather than prescribed by public guidelines. It will often require divergent thinking (identifying multiple, varied and innovative responses to a situation). The knowledge base will be largely implicational and based on multiple perspectives, but can be united by some shared underlying principles (such as a strong sense of ethics or the pursuit of a social cause). Hence, in terms of creating a Mission, therapists do not know:

- what issues, clients or groups will present for help;
- what information will be relevant to understanding the client's needs and how to go about gathering this information;
- which ethical or legal issues are likely to arise;

- who else is involved in the client's or group's life and/or care, and may need to be engaged;
- what the contract needs to be (contracts, if they exist at all, will be evolutionary and subject to multiple revisions).

Consider this type of service setting. If you were this counsellor working in this context, how would you define your Mission?

Example of working in Quadrant 4: individual and unknown.

A therapist working in a service for those undergoing life-changing events (potentially involving the need for transformational change in worldview)

This might arise in multiple contexts, including a service for those made redundant, those faced with a terminal diagnosis, or in coaching a client presented with a new role demanding an understanding well outside their existing ways of seeing the world. Within such services there is usually an established framework for offering the service and making decisions within it. However, such services are likely to be faced with situations where neither client nor counsellor has any idea what a resolution will look like, or even how to define the problem faced. Within such services there will usually be a small number of counsellors who are able to accept referrals from colleagues when those colleagues find themselves completely out of their depth.

In these circumstances, therapists cannot rely on an existing evidence base or structure the problem as an hypothesis to be tested (neither the pursuit of truth nor the pursuit of evidence is viable). They cannot know what makes sense. Thus, as the therapist seeks to shape a Mission for such a service, the use of language will be very different from that of a publicly defined service offer. Specifically, it will have to focus on what the therapist can draw from within and will be built on a sense of personal truthfulness. Integrity, not evidence, is the watchword. Implicational knowledge will be primary, but this will often emerge through processes of meaning making or presence and will draw upon the authenticity, strength and courage of both counsellor and client. Hence, in terms of creating a Mission for the service, the therapist does not know:

- if it is possible to work with the client;
- what information will be relevant to understanding the client's needs and how to go about gathering this information;
- how to establish a contract with a client (although an ethical underpinning to the work will be needed);

- whether or not any ethical or legal issues will arise;
- who else is involved in the client's life and/or care and may need to be involved.

Consider this type of service setting. If you were this counsellor working in this context, how would you define your Mission?

Exercise 16:   *How do you seek to define your Mission?*

If you completed the exercises above you considered a number of Mission possibilities. Spend some time sifting through each of the four quadrants to identify the one that is nearest to your service. Then consider the bullet points under that quadrant as they apply to your service. Reflect on them for a while, think of examples that fit and any contrary stories, but also get in touch with the *felt sense* that some of the clients you worked with generated in you. Then, using this knowledge to define and refine your Mission, complete the three-step process below:

Step 1

1. Who are you as a person?
2. What is your role in this service?
3. What makes the service meaningful or worthwhile to you?

Stay with this for a while and again allow the felt sense of that meaning to emerge.

Step 2
Now, using Gardner's mirror test (see http://www.goodwork project.org/), ask: 'What enables you to look yourself in the mirror each day and say "I did a good job"?' What does 'good' feel like?

Step 3
On the basis of that definition, consider:

1. Decisions you make that are routine and straightforward.
2. Decisions that have caused you problems.
3. A critical incident that has seriously challenged your understanding of what you are doing or your sense of being worthwhile.

List your responses in your learning log.

Step 4
Having worked through all of the above, now write your Mission state-ment. Do not worry if it is not succinct or as yet fully elaborated; you will be reworking this statement as you progress through the book. When you are confident that you have arrived at your Mission statement, con-sider the decision-making models that you have available to you. Also consider the extent to which they are congruent with your defined Mis-sion. Are there gaps? If so, how might you fill them?

What is my Mission?

The previous exercises started a process of looking at your Mission and subjecting this definition to a series of reflections. Using that work pro-vides a good starting point for further reflections. We encourage you to look at the question differently, more deeply and widely (remember the ideas we looked at in Chapter 3) and in a more complex way. In this section, we invite you to elaborate that process of reflection using a frame-work that comes from a discipline very different from psychotherapy and counselling – the world of acting.

The actor, director and theorist of performance Konstantin Stanislavski (1863–1938) wrote a series of books on the actor preparing for a role. We believe that a number of his ideas have parallels in counselling and psychotherapy. As a result, and with a view to elaborating your under-standing of Mission, we provide a brief introduction to the Stanislavski system and then offer some exercises arising from it. (We draw on translations and interpretations from Lewis 1986; Benedetti 1999; and Merlin 2003.)

At the centre of Stanislavski's work is the concept of the *super objective*. This brings together all the elements, including the text, the actors and the director, to form a shared purpose. We can treat this as an analogy for the Mission described in this chapter in that all parties involved share a common purpose (in the context of theatrical performance, this is to serve the audience and the play; see Scales and West 2010).

Second is Stanislavski's notion of *interior and exterior work* – the inner creative state (psychological work on self and character), the external cre-ative state (technical and physical work), and understanding of the 'given circumstances' or context which governs the performance. This brings to-gether all the perspectives that will inform our work together. The analogy is with Attitude as we use it here (see Chapter 6).

Third is the exploration and movement from work on self and the super objective to self in role and performance – what Stanislavski calls the *through line of action*. The analogy for us is with Process.

To make the parallel explicit, if we think about ourselves preparing for our role as therapist we can understand this task as one of:

- finding and agreeing the *super objective* for the work (the Mission);
- undertaking the *interior and exterior work* to prepare us (developing the appropriate stance and Attitude);
- undertaking the endeavour of moving from work on self through to the performance with our clients in the context of the encounter with the client – the *through line of action* (the Process).

In using the Stanislavski system we need to revisit the Mission statement so far constructed in the light of his additional questions, presented below. Working with the version of your Mission statement from Exercise 16, complete the next exercise.

Exercise 17: *Establishing the super objective for your role as therapist*

1. Read your Mission statement (preferably out loud). What is the core narrative, or essential theme, without which the story does not make sense – what Callow (2010) defines as the 'insistent question'?
2. Once you have answered that 'insistent question', identify the actors in the story. (In therapy, we would prefer the term 'clients'.) What is their contribution to the super objective?
3. Who are the directors for this story? This includes gatekeepers and any collective guidelines (handed down by 'directors') to which you must adhere. What is their contribution to the super objective?
4. Now consider those comprising your audience (it may not be just the client sitting in front of you). What is their contribution to the super objective?
5. Finally, consider whether it is possible to write a shared narrative (i.e. develop a super objective) that ties all the elements together. If it is possible, try writing it down and keep reading the different versions out loud until one resonates with you and has a felt sense of truthfulness.

Once you have a version that resonates, you are probably close to a reworked Mission statement.

Some definitions of Mission

So far we have argued that it is essential for practitioners to understand their professional context, and the circumstances that influence their practice. This provides a basis for developing a personalized, successful decision-making approach. In this section we offer two (of many potential) illustrations of this. The first looks at a Mission within the individual unknown quadrant and the second the collective unknown quadrant.

David's log. Example of a Mission within the individual unknown quadrant

On 11 September 2001, I received a call from one of my clients. She asked if I was watching the television, which I was. In her organization, a trading company, the screens were permanently switched on. Staff members in London saw, as they happened, the attacks on the World Trade Center in New York, in one tower of which their colleagues were based. She asked if I could get to London immediately to discuss how we might set up a support system in what was a very chaotic situation.

We were facing a situation which contained elements of the known; terrorist attacks were not new, but this was of such magnitude that it was beyond most people's experience. It was also a mass attack that was witnessed as it happened across the world, with messages from inside the Towers emerging in real time and colleagues, friends and relatives seeing the destruction of their loved ones played over and over again. While I had had experience of other disaster situations, and had written on the matter as well as provided trauma counselling services, this was the first time I had seen and heard the unfolding story alongside those I would be helping. On arriving in London, it was clear that many individuals had been deeply affected as they personally knew many working in the Twin Towers. They had both to deal with their emotions and fears, and to make decisions which had significant business and market consequences.

The organization was clear that it wanted to do whatever was most appropriate for their staff, and looked to me to assess the situation, and to devise and implement a planned response. However, there was no agreed collective framework for such a service. We were all on an individual journey from the unknown.

What might the Mission be here? How might you have developed the Mission in this situation? Here is what actually occurred.

David's response

Initially, it seemed that a super objective might be quickly found. The organization stated that it wanted to do what was best for the staff and I certainly wanted to devise a worthwhile response. What was most appropriate was unclear, given the circumstances and how much of the situation was unknown. Dealing with personal reactions while still needing to make business decisions represented the first potential conflict. Where do you look for answers in known evidence bases in order to create a structured decision model?

The literature on disaster management had developed rapidly over the previous few years from a low base in the 1980s to significant research by this time. During the late 1980s and early 1990s a model of practice had grown up which combined counselling and critical incident debriefing initially, with longer-term work to alleviate post-traumatic stress disorder (PTSD) where necessary. However, by the late 1990s this research was being challenged and elements of it were seen by some as unhelpful or harmful, while still being championed by others. As a result, the literature did not lend itself well to a structured decision-making model and, in fact, added to the confusion. In terms of the organization, the response was highly varied, some seemingly minimally affected and others significantly so. The organization had to function, closure was not a considered option, and the work for staff during that period was intense. After multiple conversations conducted over two days, a shared sense emerged which could form the basis for a Mission statement.

The elements included:

1. To support staff in the immediate aftermath of the incident to continue functioning in their role, and to support those who did not feel able to do so without prejudice to their position; to provide management debriefing across the organization to allow issues that needed to be addressed to emerge and enable decision-making to address these; to support managers in dealing with their own responses while providing structures to help them support their staff.
2. Following the immediate response, to set up continued debriefing and counselling as needed so that the staff could feel fully recovered and in the longer term seek to mitigate continuing impacts. The whole framework was to be kept under review and adjusted as circumstances changed.

In terms of the disaster literature, a decision model for the response, recovery and mitigation phases was established (Taylor and Lane 1991). This included structured decision models where the literature supported it (for example, debriefing sheets were provided and counselling services established). It also included emergent decision-making models to respond to rapidly changing circumstances; a short decision chain was set up so that different modifications to service could be introduced as needed. A senior manager was assigned to liaise with the support team daily, with authority to assess and decide.

David's log. Example of a Mission within the collective unknown quadrant

This case example provides a different and more complex illustration of how a Mission might emerge, based on work I carried out during the 1970s. Here, the focus was on establishing an educational guidance centre in a political context of increasing concern about levels of disruptive behaviour in the school system. Schools (particularly secondary schools) were seen as facing a crisis caused by unruly children lacking parental discipline. In the period shortly after the raising of the school leaving age from 15 to 16 years, schools had struggled to find ways to engage children now required to remain in education when previously they could leave. The response at a national level was to fund projects to deal with disruption. At a local level, influenced by the views of teachers, many projects emerged which removed children from school into off-site centres where supposedly they could be taught to behave and be returned to school 'reformed'. In practice, few children returned and the centres became, for many, alternative sites of education. A backlash later occurred as a disproportionate number of ethnic-minority children filled these places and so were effectively excluded from school. Such centres were seen by some as a means of social control.

On being appointed to direct one of these centres, I was instructed that the identified purpose was to accept referrals of difficult secondary children, remove them from school for a few months and then return them reformed. The 'shadow story' was that they were unlikely to be so, although that could not be openly stated. The evidence for the failure of these initiatives was already emerging at a time when nationally there was a rush to open many more (Her Majesty's Inspectorate 1978). There was a collective agreed position

at a local as well as national level that provided a structure for this type of service.
(This section is taken from Corrie and Lane (2010), where a more detailed description can be found.)

Before reading on, how might you have set out to define the Mission for this service? Here is what actually occurred.

David's response

Between appointment and opening the centre, I had the opportunity to talk with many of the key stakeholders, including my employer, teachers, other professionals, inspectors, parents and the children themselves. What came to light were multiple accounts which did not necessarily fit the authorized version. Thus, different stories began to unfold. For example, a number of head teachers at primary schools argued that, rather than placing all the emphasis on secondary pupils out of school, it would be preferable to work with primary school children before they reached the point of exclusion.

From these multiple accounts, a key theme emerged – namely that working in schools with teachers and children with additional part-time support out of school was preferable to removing children from school. The Mission could be renegotiated based on the shared narrative (or super objective) from a centre which received excluded children to one that provided a school-focused service to enhance inclusion. Multiple conflicting objectives existed in the community, and building the shared narrative was necessary to create a super objective that could provide the basis for an agreed Mission. In this case, had a structured model been applied, a very different Mission would have been imposed on the client group. By allowing a process of dialogue, different decisions became possible.

How might you have developed the Mission in this situation given this additional information? You might like to consider if any of the narratives above have any thing to say to the Mission statement you have just written and read out loud. (If you are curious about why we asked you to read it out loud to check that it resonated, you will find the answer in Chapter 7, or by reading Stanislavski's work.)

Conclusion

Being clear about the Mission that underpins your work with clients supports you in making decisions relating to the early phases of therapy.

It is concerned with the decisions that frame initial contact, including whether contact with a client proceeds beyond a referral letter or the initial consultation, and, if undertaken, moves on to engagement, ending and follow-up. Your Mission statement also facilitates decision-making by alerting you to the dilemmas you are likely to face and the variety of frameworks that you have to draw upon.

In this chapter we have sought to explore the development of your Mission to provide the starting point for creating models for decision-making that are appropriate to your context. We have provided a number of exercises which draw upon the decision literature but have also taken you beyond this to an earlier tradition in the arts. We have introduced the idea that decisions might be made where data are known, unknown or unknowable. Sometimes there are areas where a structured process has more or less value. We have also looked at the area of individual and collective decision-making and how your Mission might be situated in different quadrants requiring alternative decision models.

We started this chapter by suggesting that you would be able to:

- reflect on the relevance of a coherent Mission to your own learning, practice and development as a therapist;
- define your own Mission, and structure what you bring to decision-making situations with your clients.

Having been introduced to these processes, we offered a number of exercises which we hope have enabled you to think reflectively and intuitively about your Mission. In doing so, you have drawn upon different decision-making systems that can help you create your own Mission statement that will be of value to you and your clients. This will prepare you for the next phase in building a decision model – an exploration of the optimum Attitude.

✍ Learning summary

One idea I have found useful in this chapter is. . .

....

....

One thing I would like to experiment with, having read this chapter, is. . .

....

....

Was there anything I didn't quite understand? (If so, I will find out more by. . .)

....

....

6 Identifying the Attitude that informs your decisions

In this chapter you will learn about:

- the Attitude which organizes your thinking about clients' needs
- three different perspectives or 'fields of vision' through which you can navigate your decision-making with, and about, clients
- how to improve your decision-making in relation to your Attitude

By reading this chapter you will be able to:

- appreciate how your perspectives shape your approach to working with clients
- identify the main perspectives that have informed your work
- critically evaluate your Attitude to help you develop a more systematic, collaborative and ultimately effective approach

---

Introduction

Over the course of professional training, we assimilate many Attitudes[1] that are deemed to be exemplars of 'good practice'. A number of these are assimilated consciously and willingly through in-depth study and critical analysis. For example, immersing oneself in the theoretical contributions of psychoanalysis, receiving formal training and supervision in this approach, and undergoing one's own analysis are likely to result in our learning to think about clients' needs from this particular perspective. Equally, if we choose this professional pathway for ourselves we are likely to retain an awareness that our beliefs about the clients we encounter will be shaped by these experiences.

Other Attitudes will be acquired indirectly through exposure to a wide range of more subtle influences. These are likely to include the values and beliefs operating in the field of professional practice, wider societal beliefs about the contribution of therapy to people's lives and the impact of living and working in a particular culture at a specific point in history. These perspectives, as we saw in Chapter 2, will give rise to certain 'foundational assumptions' which have been absorbed through more subtle means and which, although critical in shaping our contribution, are not readily open to introspection. In other words, it is easy to uncritically assimilate attitudes from external sources which we have not consciously chosen but which nonetheless influence how we work with clients in critical ways (Baxter Magolda 2009).

If you are going to navigate the decision-making procedures of the service in which you are working, you need to be aware of the legacy that your context has given you. This chapter is concerned with better understanding those factors that influence the expectations of therapist and client, and inform how the therapy unfolds.

We begin by helping you reflect on some of the major influences that have shaped your thinking and, in particular, the perspectives that guide your approach to working with clients. These influences can be seen as perspectives, or 'fields of vision', through which you operate. We then present three distinct perspectives – the personal, interpersonal and systemic – and examine how identifying which one you are operating in can help you navigate the decision-making frameworks described in this book. Drawing on Stanislavski's model, discussed in the previous chapter, we explore how this navigation relies on both the technical preparation you undertake at the level of theory and skills development and the psychological preparation you undertake to be able to work safely in your service context. In considering these contexts we will ask you to relate this back to the different quadrants outlined in the Mission chapter and how your preparation (development of Attitude) has enabled you to work within them.

Understanding the perspectives that shape who we are: a message from history

In 1910, the German politician Clara Zetkin proposed the establishment of an International Women's Day as a means of campaigning against gender inequality. At that time, women were campaigning for the right to vote and for greater participation in the work place. The subsequent increase in the active participation and contribution of women was the result of a range of factors. However, few would doubt that a major contribution was the ongoing battles of those committed to the women's suffrage movement.

Sarah's log

Researching this anniversary led me to revisit the 'privileges' to which many women are now entitled, including the right to be educated, to vote and to own property, to have a career of their own choosing, to express their sexuality and to have male colleagues and friends with whom they can spend time (without a chaperone).

These privileges are not shared among all women in all cultures, and it is important to remember the inequalities that remain. However, as a woman living and working in the UK at this point in history, these entitlements permeate how I define myself, my service offer to clients and the way in which I conceptualize and approach personal development work. Although I rarely state them explicitly to my colleagues or clients, these beliefs and values represent a lens, or field of vision, through which I view the world and approach the work that I label 'therapy'. It is my inheritance from the men and women who came before me.

However much we might like to see ourselves as independent thinkers, we cannot extricate our capacity to think, judge and make decisions from the historical and cultural contexts in which we are embedded. Although I can intellectually understand the views of the women in Britain who saw the actions of the suffragettes as going against the laws of nature, I cannot function from this perspective. My own cultural and historical context has closed down the capacity to make decisions, to judge and to act from this perspective.

Our perspectives, and the collective contexts in which certain beliefs are formed and maintained, have important implications for our work as therapists. For example, in considering the reasons why, in western culture, depression is increasingly depicted as an illness, Martell et al. (2001) highlight how our society has a strong culture of blame, tending to hold individuals responsible for the difficulties that befall them. In such a culture, the label of illness or disease is likely to result in more sympathetic responses from others, as well as affording access to benefits, 'treatment' and other forms of support.

In contrast, when people are held accountable (i.e. responsible) for their difficulties, society is more likely to respond with negative judgement and blame. Martell et al. (2001) highlight one particularly problematic manifestation of this cultural Attitude in relation to individuals living with HIV and AIDS. Here, those affected have all too easily been labelled as either innocent victims (babies born HIV positive, or individuals exposed to the virus through blood transfusions) or irresponsible and somehow deserving of the fate that has befallen them (such as sexually active gay men, drug users and sex workers).

A commonly encountered variation of the 'culture of blame' at work in the therapist's consulting room is the client who, coming to therapy following referral from a medical practitioner, expresses relief at having been diagnosed as depressed. By being given the label of illness, they no longer see themselves as blameworthy. In the language of attribution theory (see Chapter 1), medical advice has enabled them to shift their self-judgement from an internal attribution (one of weakness, failure or incompetence) to an external attribution (illness/disease). Perhaps partly for this reason, therapists are increasingly called upon to provide 'disorder-specific' models of 'treatment'; in our culture, illness is the respectable face of human distress.

Interestingly, a new Attitude may also be emerging. Whereas the stigma associated with mental health problems has long been acknowledged, it has also been reported that a growing number of individuals actually *want* a diagnosis of mental illness – albeit of a particular kind. For example, in a BBC news article Dr Diana Chan (2010) reported how bipolar disorder has increased in popularity as a self-diagnostic label, and proposed that this may reflect the willingness of celebrities to talk about their own experiences of mental health problems. When associated with individuals who are seen as creative, intelligent and successful, there is the potential for bipolar disorder to be seen as a fashionable label that denotes creativity and aspirations to higher social status by association with the celebrities who have been similarly diagnosed.

The important point here is not, of course, whether categories of human distress do or do not constitute illnesses, but rather that the individual perspectives we hold are immersed in social, cultural and historical perspectives and that it is impossible – for ourselves as well as our clients – to remain wholly outside their sphere of influence.

Enhancing awareness of your own perspectives

Regardless of where we are on our career journey, we all have sources of influence that have shaped us and of which it would be useful to be aware. Paul and Elder (2002) suggest that if we wish to enhance our capacity as decision-makers and critical thinkers, we must first examine the foundations of our thinking so that we can identify at least some of the 'ingredients' that have led us to think as we do. Adapting the factors that they suggest are important to consider, answer the following questions to help you clarify those 'fields of vision' that that have shaped your own thinking:

Exercise 18:   *Identifying the factors that have shaped your Perspective*

- What historical period were you born into? What opportunities and constraints have been afforded you as a result of being born into this period of time? (If you are not sure, consider how your options and views on the world may have been different if you had been born 50 years ago, 100 years ago or 200 years ago.)
- What culture(s) were you born into? What are some of the values and beliefs central to this (these) culture(s)? (If you are not sure, consider how your view of yourself, others and life would be different if you had been born into a very different culture.)
- In your formative years, what were the major political, economic and social challenges (both local and global) that were occurring? (For example, did you grow up during a time of relative national economic prosperity or was the country in recession? Was it a period of rampant materialism, or a period in which the country's faith in materialism was shaken? Which political party was in power and how did that shape the social, economic and political outlook of the time?)
- What type of family were you born into? What were the beliefs, values, circumstances and behaviour of those around you? What did you learn about how to conduct yourself in the world, how to relate to others and how to achieve what you want?
- Into which peer groups were you initiated? What were the dominant values, rules and codes of conduct of these peer groups? What was your place within these peer groups and what 'fields of vision' might you have inherited from them?

Spend some time engaging with these questions. They are deceptively simple and will enable you to uncover much more about yourself and your approach to being a therapist than you might imagine on initial reading. See if you can begin to identify how these experiences may have given rise to certain perspectives that shape how you view your service to clients generally, and the way in which you make sense of clients' needs specifically. Your responses will provide a personal context for thinking about the different perspectives in the next section. It is part of your psychological preparation for the role of therapist.

Perspectives on human experience, human distress and therapeutic change

As therapists we are presented with an often bewildering array of theories, models and techniques that can lead us to feel unclear about what is needed in a particular instance. Should you aim to modify a problematic cognition, target behavioural change or work at the level of feelings? Can you achieve the desired outcome by working with the individual, or will it be necessary to work with the client and their family? Does the solution lie in promoting greater insight and offering tools for change, or is the client in need of benefits, housing and other forms of state-levied support?

When attempting to identify the Attitude that influences how we approach our work with clients, we would be justified in considering different theories of personality, beliefs about the 'causes' of human difficulties and different ideas about what constitutes acceptable evidence of change. Each explanation from psychology, psychotherapy and counselling positions itself differently in relation to what constitutes distress and helping and does, therefore, generate a different set of decisions that must be made. Each perspective enables and constrains the types of explanations and methods permitted according to the parameters it defines. So, for example, when therapists are guided by a diagnostic approach derived from the medical model, their decision-making will be greatly influenced by the symptomatic aspects of their clients' experience which are likely to be privileged over social and economic factors. Decisions made will be tied closely to whether the symptom profile 'matches' one particular diagnostic category better than another, and how to address dilemmas (e.g. what to do if a client appears to have certain characteristics typical of a diagnosis, but not others).

Despite a range of potential explanations available to us, there is no over-arching theory or model that can adequately account for the diverse facets of human experience we encounter in the consulting room. Lazare (1976) highlighted how we are simultaneously biological organisms, psychological selves, behaving animals and members of social systems.

Depending on our views, we might also add that we are spiritual beings and members of political and cultural systems. Although it is possible to debate the relative contribution of these domains to an individual's request for help, each would, to a large extent, be recognized by all health care professionals.

Lazare (1976) proposes that, given human beings' multidimensional nature, therapists need a multidimensional approach to assessment, in which psychological, social, biological and behavioural hypotheses are generated and tested in a systematic fashion. A framework such as this offers many benefits. In particular, it has the potential to improve quality of care through preventing the therapist from arriving at premature conclusions whilst ensuring an efficient use of time. What is also important about Lazare's model is that it highlights how therapists need a framework for thinking about the different perspectives on change.

In previous work (see Lane and Corrie 2006; Corrie and Lane 2010) we described a useful framework for navigating the different perspectives on change. Specifically, we suggested that the dominant therapeutic approaches available to us for thinking about our clients' needs (humanistic, existential, psychodynamic, behavioural, cognitive, systemic, solution-focused, etc.) can be categorized according to one of three broad types of explanation: the *personal*, the *interpersonal* and the *systemic* (Figure 2). Each of these perspectives orients us in how we listen to our clients' stories, permeates our therapeutic understanding of clients' needs and informs our decision-making in critical ways.

These perspectives on change are perhaps best understood as distinct fields of vision that shape or even determine our decision-making

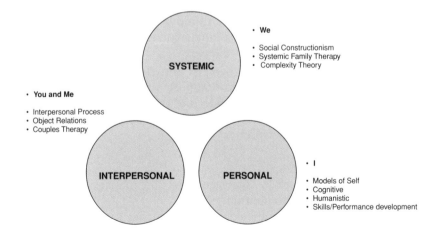

Figure 2 Perspectives on change

capability in a given situation. They are part of our technical preparation for the role of therapist. However, working within these fields also draws upon our sense of self. We will feel more or less comfortable in each of them. For some it feels easier to work in one area (e.g. the cognitive within the personal field) and uncomfortable in another (family therapy within the systemic). Recognizing our preferences is part of our psychological preparation for the role. Each may draw upon not only different theory but also other skills and potentially deeper levels of connectedness to our sense of self. We now consider each of these in turn.

The personal perspective

When we operate from the personal perspective, we are concerned with what each person brings to the consultation as a starting point. This includes individual beliefs about self, other, the process of therapy and prospects for change which have the potential to influence any decision-making that subsequently takes place. Key influences will stem from:

- the therapist's beliefs about therapy (remember the schema you uncovered in Chapter 1);
- the client's beliefs about therapy;
- the therapist's personal journey through life (examined earlier in this chapter);
- the client's personal journey through life;
- the therapist's epistemology and ontology (including that acquired through personal experience, training and professional development);
- the client's epistemology and ontology (including that acquired through personal and professional experience).

These perspectives will orient therapist and client to pursuing therapeutic interventions focused on those aspects of the client's difficulties that are potentially more directly under the individual's control. In the fields of therapy and personal development, there are a number of models which prize the personal perspective, including:

- cognitive therapies;
- skills training (such as assertiveness or time management);
- neuro-linguistic programming (NLP);
- biological explanations (such as those used in systems of psychiatric diagnosis and classification and the medical model more broadly).

These models are essentially operating in the known quadrants which we explored in Chapter 5. They might be used in service contexts that are collective or individual, but they all assume linear cause–effect relationships. The following case study provides an example of how therapist and client might work together from the personal field of vision.

Sarah's log. Treating Richard's panic disorder

Following the sudden onset of frightening physical sensations that included palpitations, tingling in his fingers and toes, chest pain and dry mouth, Richard had been referred for a psychiatric assessment. Having assessed him, and aware that a full medical examination carried out by his GP had excluded other illnesses, the psychiatrist explained that Richard was experiencing panic attacks and diagnosed him as having panic disorder without agoraphobia. My colleague explained to Richard how sensations of panic are associated with the 'fight or flight' response and that he could be helped to make changes in these distressing sensations. Richard, who was otherwise very satisfied with his life, felt great relief that he was neither physically ill nor going mad.

The psychiatrist referred Richard to see me. We discussed the potential benefits of a course of cognitive behaviour therapy aimed at helping Richard understand what was occurring in his body when he experienced panic attacks, and then helping him find ways to test out some of his catastrophic fears in order to bring about change. Therapy proceeded very smoothly. Eight sessions later, Richard no longer believed that experiencing a panic attack meant he was seriously ill or going mad, and the inexplicable physical sensations that had once caused him such fear gradually ceased altogether.

This is a good example of an approach to change derived from the personal perspective. Both Richard's psychiatrist and therapist understood his difficulties in the context of medical (physical sensations that met diagnostic criteria for panic disorder without agoraphobia) and psychological (catastrophic misinterpretation of his bodily sensations) explanations and conveyed this to Richard in a way that had validity for him. An approach to change that originated from the personal perspective (identifying and testing out catastrophic predictions) was also highly acceptable to Richard as it fitted with his active and goal-focused approach to life. Both the client's difficulty and the professionals' proposed response to it centred on aspects of the client's internal world that could be identified, examined and ultimately changed to bring about a positive result.

When working from within the personal perspective, therapists' decisions are likely to be closely connected with an in-depth explanation of phenomena that are experienced and disclosed by the client, including:

- feelings;
- thoughts, assumptions and beliefs;
- rules for living and personal values;
- images;
- sensations and body states;
- heritability (e.g. genetic potential, such as strong family history of a particular disorder or disability);
- experiences that can be categorized as symptoms.

Within this sphere accurate decision-making (see Chapter 1) becomes vital. For example, if a therapist is devising and implementing an intervention based on the assumption that the client has panic disorder, and their approach is informed by the latest research evidence relating to that disorder, it is no good if the client is actually suffering from obsessive-compulsive disorder where the symptom profile requires a different type of intervention.

Think about a time when you worked with a client from the personal perspective. What was helpful about this? What, if anything, was less helpful about it? What assumptions are you making when you operate from this perspective, and how do these filter through into your decision-making?

The interpersonal perspective

When we think about interpersonal perspectives, we are concerned with how therapist and client might each be shaped by the encounter that unfolds between them, how the client is embedded in a wide variety of one-to-one relationships and how decision-making needs to take account of the impact of these. It is important to emphasize here that this does not relate to the therapist's level of attunement to their client's experience – therapists operating within the personal perspective will be sensitive to their own and their client's moment-to-moment reactions to the material of the session. Rather, the interpersonal field of vision is concerned with beliefs about how transformation takes place and the foundational assumption that this is deeply and irrevocably bound to the relational. For example, the philosopher and theologian Martin Buber (e.g. 1937) emphasized the notion of the 'encounter' between the 'I' and the 'thou'.

A true encounter between persons, he claims, is where the other person is experienced without labels or bounds and is therefore connected to everything. Buber argues that, in contrast, many of our everyday interactions with others feature as 'I–it' relationships, whereby others are perceived as essentially object, as separate from oneself. For Buber, 'life is meeting' and healing comes in and through relationship.

Equally, attachment theory (Bowlby 1988) describes the critical necessity of having a 'secure base' that enables us to develop an internal working model of relationships and that our capacity for relationship or 'relationality' begins in the mother's womb; we are biologically 'hard-wired' for relationship (Righetti et al. 2005). Attachment theory is not a model of therapy. However, in her work on relational trauma, Jordan (2010) highlights how awareness of this literature, and drawing in particular on attachment theory to promote healing in the client's attachment system, can strengthen therapeutic work, especially given the importance of the quality of the therapeutic relationship to therapeutic outcome.

An example of the interpersonal perspective from an evolutionary perspective is sociometer theory (Leary 1999) and its contribution to understanding low self-esteem. Sociometer theory proposes that self-esteem originally served an evolutionary function as a monitor of social acceptance. Its function was not to maintain self-esteem for its own sake (because having robust self-esteem makes us feel good, for example). Rather, it provides cues that tell us whether or not we are adequately valued and accepted by others – and if not, prompts us to adopt relationship-enhancing behaviours. Earlier in our evolutionary history, this ability would have been essential to our survival prospects. For example, by being able to gauge the extent to which they were included or excluded by their social group, individuals were potentially able to avoid the social devaluation and rejection that might have resulted in expulsion from the community, with potentially disastrous consequences for their survival chances.

This field of vision is likely to orient therapist and client to pursuing questions, decisions and therapeutic interventions that are focused on the aspects that emerge from the interactions between self and other. Models which might be said to prize the relational include:

- couples therapy;
- psychodynamic psychotherapy, in particular object relations theories;
- behavioural and contingent ways of working;
- models which consider the essential social and context-dependent nature of self and action (e.g. Gestalt therapy).

Sarah's log: Helping Sally and Tom rewrite their future

Sally and Tom had been working with me for several months trying to understand and resolve their marital difficulties. Sally argued that Tom failed to show sufficient sensitivity to her needs, angry that he spent much of his spare time at the pub. Tom argued that Sally's nagging was driving him away and that she should appreciate his contribution more than she did (he worked hard for his family and always took up offers of overtime to make sure he was bringing in a good wage). At the time of referral Tom and Sally were contemplating a separation but were anxious about the impact on their four children, all of whom were under 10. Both Tom and Sally came from violent family backgrounds, where their parents had separated after years of arguments and, in Tom's case, physical abuse of his mother at the hands of his father. They both wondered whether, because of their backgrounds, their marriage was also doomed to failure.

My assessment was that given their upbringings, neither Sally nor Tom had had effective marital communications modelled for them. Nor had they had the opportunity to acquire effective listening and problem-solving skills. My hypothesis was that the 'tug of war' which existed between them was the result of interpersonal exchanges that reflected these difficulties.

Making it very clear that I held neither party 'responsible' for the couple's difficulties but was simply looking for ways of introducing a change to see what effect it might have, I asked Sally if she would consider trying a different approach when Tom returned home from the pub. Instead of making her disapproval felt by shouting at him, I asked Sally is she could smile at him, give him a hug and ask him about his day – even if it felt counter-intuitive to do so. After some hesitation and much discussion, Sally agreed. After a month of trying out this behaviour, the effect was significant. On one occasion, Tom invited Sally to come to the pub with him (something he had never done before) and started coming home earlier in the evenings. Although it wasn't always possible for Sally to sustain this, and this was only one small part of the work that was to take place, Sally and Tom learnt something important, namely, that it was possible to steer their relationship in a different direction and to get a different reaction from their partner by altering their own behaviour. Their future did not have to be dictated by their family history...

When working from the interpersonal perspective, decisions are likely to focus on the client's responses to questions associated with:

- working with the moment-to-moment interactions between therapist and client(s), or client and others – whether framed in terms of an 'I–thou' encounter, interpersonal processes or transference and counter-transference interpretations.
- the antecedents and consequences of a particular behaviour, and how our clients' actions (even those judged to be maladaptive) can be seen to serve a function when understood in context. This includes attention to the contexts in which a particular behaviour does and does not occur.
- attachment theory, including whether or not the client was enabled to develop a 'secure base' that could enable the development of a stable sense of self.
- the evolutionary context of particular profiles of response (internal and external) and how these might, at some point in our evolutionary history, have served to regulate attachment relationships, interpersonal bonding and security within one's social group.

Because of these factors, when we are working within this field of vision, we often need to look beyond the issue of accuracy that we examined in Chapter 1. Here, some of the factors we identified in Chapter 2 become paramount, such as how the client might be held in the 'grip' of a powerful, detrimental story from the past (and may need to 'rewrite' the story), what is possible for a client at a specific point in time (as opposed to what is technically accurate), or how we find a type of language to connect with a client (potentially, the language of story-telling and metaphor or drawing upon other implicational forms of knowledge in an attempt to enter into their world). In a therapeutic relationship that is reparative, and that can provide the vehicle for transformation and healing, decisions about the timing and pacing of questions, interpretations and interventions are also critical.

Think about a time when you worked with a client from the interpersonal perspective. What was helpful about this? What, if anything, was less helpful about it? What assumptions are you making when you operate from this perspective, and how do these filter through into your decision-making?

The systemic perspective

If you completed Exercise 18 earlier in this chapter, you will already have a good understanding of some of the historical, social and cultural factors that have shaped the Attitude you bring to your work with clients. As therapists we, just like our clients, are immersed in systems that influence the ways we think and operate. Much of the time those influences are beyond our awareness.

A systems perspective resists the notion that the causes of problems can be located within an individual – whether framed in terms of personality type, thoughts, feelings or symptom profile. Rather, it considers how individuals' dilemmas might be a function of the system(s) in which they find themselves. In systemic therapy, for example, the problems experienced by an individual would be understood as a product of family relationships, with symptoms representing problems in communication between members rather than reflections of a member's underlying illness.

O'Neill (2007) uses the analogy of a spider's web to describe the functioning of the system, or 'social interactional field', that shapes an individual's actions. Specifically, she highlights how when any organism makes contact with any part of the web, the entire web moves. The web can (up to a point) withstand strain on its multiple strands and maintain its structural integrity through a range of conditions that are significantly greater than its own weight (weather, insects, etc.). Likewise, she proposes that an interactional field established by a system (involving two or more people) will have its own strengths, anchor points, 'structural integrity' and breaking point. When any member within the social interactional field, or system, moves, the other members experience the impact – as such the system shapes the actions and reactions of the person requesting help, which in turn shapes the responses of others.

When working within the systemic perspective, therapists' decisions are likely to be closely connected with a broader range of influencing factors including, potentially, explanations couched within wider social, economic and political factors that impact on the client's life and the therapist's ability to support them. Here, we might consider:

- the context in which the client's problem emerged (when and how it emerged, who noticed and who was most affected);
- the relative influence of the client's immediate and extended family, including beliefs about problems and how they should be addressed;
- the client's social, political and economic circumstances and status;
- membership of mainstream and/or marginalized social groups;
- political factors around access to education and health care;
- the current political and economic climate in which our service is provided.

Of course, this raises the question of which systems need to be considered. For example, is it those directly connected to the client and which may be open to direct influence, such as a partner, family members or colleagues? Or do we need to consider those indirectly connected to the client but which shape the context in which you work together (e.g. the Mission statement of the service, risk assessment policies, or the priorities of the referrer – such as a psychological report requested by a solicitor as part of a compensation claim)? Or is it influences that are distal to the client, such as social, economic, political factors that are unlikely to be directly open to impact? (For example, the client may be refused a service on the basis of new, streamlined referral criteria in response to cutbacks in public sector funding stemming from government policy.)

There are a number of ways in which we can approach our work when operating from within the systemic perspective. At the level of therapeutic intervention, for example, systemic family therapy provides a social perspective on the origins of difficulties and the factors that maintain them (White and Epston 1990; Dallos and Draper 2005). In contrast, Lane and Corrie (2006; see also Corrie and Lane 2010) have argued for the need to distinguish the impact of local, national and global influences on our engagement with clients. Local influences refer to the beliefs, values, codes of ethics and decision-making procedures operating internally to a particular service setting, training scheme or governing professional body. National influences refer to the ideology of the political party in power that informs policy development and shapes public expectation, the state of the national economy, broader social, cultural and political priorities and the prevailing views of human nature dominant within society. Global influences are concerned with international trends in welfare or the delivery of health and social care (concerns affecting the global community, including wider social, political and economic factors).

Because of these factors, when we are working within this perspective, we need to look beyond the issue of accuracy that we examined in Chapter 1 and the different styles of reasoning that we discussed in Chapter 2. Here, some of the models and decision-making frameworks that we described in Chapter 3 become paramount. For example, we need to appreciate that many of the challenges we and our clients confront are occurring in situations of complexity that do not lend themselves well to structured, linear approaches to decision-making – the known quadrants that we examined in Chapter 5. We need to recognize that we operate in different spaces within which certain types of decision and ways of working become viable and others less so. We need to consider whether we are operating in the rational space, the emergent space or the chaotic space and whether, as a result, we need to bring a different, deeper, wider or more complex perspective to our decision-making approach (see Chapter 3). We have to decide if we need to address the unknown and in doing so prepare ourselves for the anxiety that must be contained in highly ambiguous contexts.

Thinking and working effectively at a systemic level entails some complex mental operations. Early in your career, especially during initial training, it is often appropriate to anchor your decision-making primarily within the personal, and possibly interpersonal, perspectives. If this is the level at which you are working, then we would recommend that you simply hold in mind any systemic influences and reflect on how they might impact your practice at a more distant level.

If, however, you find yourself working with clients in complex circumstances or are providing therapy to clients in organizations that are undergoing significant amounts of upheaval and reconfiguration, you may want to know more about how to understand organizational change using systems theory. If you are in this position, it will be essential for you to consider whether you are psychologically and technically prepared for this type of work. You will also need to consider the adequacy of the supervisory and support structures available to you. If you are not prepared, or the support structures are not in place, explore options to refer the client elsewhere. Your supervisor will be able to guide you with this.

One way to begin developing sensitivity to systemic issues is to notice your thoughts, feelings and actions in different places. If you find yourself reacting in very different ways this may, O'Neill (2007) suggests, reflect the interactional fields of these different organizations. Other questions that can be useful for identifying systemic influences include the following:

- Do people seem happy working in your service?
- What is the staff turnover like?
- What is the service's sickness record like?
- How are the clients talked about?
- Are members of the team able to express doubt and uncertainty in their practice?
- How does the service attempt to protect its boundaries?
- Do you feel good being there?

If you have already had the opportunity to work at a systems level, think about a time when you worked with a client from a systemic perspective (examples of work where this may occur include family therapy; indirect work such as working with staff in a care home in order to improve quality of life for a dementia sufferer; a piece of consultancy work for a service or executive coaching). What was helpful about this? What, if anything, was less helpful about it? What assumptions are you making when you operate from this perspective, and how do these filter through into your decision-making? If you have not worked at this level, what do you imagine might be some of the opportunities and challenges that arise for a practitioner from working within a systems perspective?

Exercise 19:   *Which field of vision is dominant for you?*

Spend some time thinking about your practice with clients to date. Of the three perspectives discussed in this chapter – the personal, interpersonal and systemic – which one tends to dominate your thinking about clients' difficulties and needs? Can you identify some of the factors that might have influenced the development of your preference? Then think about a recent situation with a client where you needed to make a decision and ask yourself the following questions:

- What was the decision that you needed to make?
- Through which perspective did you view the decision that needed to be made – personal, interpersonal or systemic? (If systemic, is this a proximal or distal system?)
- Within this perspective, which direction did you choose to follow (e.g. a particular therapeutic approach or method of intervention)? What did you gain and lose through this choice?
- Whose agenda was served by this work?
- Who and what was involved in shaping the decision you made?
- Which factors were most influential in shaping your decision?
- Which factors were least influential in shaping your decision?
- Who benefited most from the decision that was made? Who, if anyone, lost out?
- What were the goals that sat behind or underpinned your decision (what values, beliefs or intended outcomes did they reflect)?
- What might have been enabled for your client by taking a different stance?

Conclusion

Regardless of where we are on our career journey, we all have sources of influence that have shaped us. If you are going to make better decisions, you need to recognize the legacy that your context has given you. Arguably, much of psychotherapy has operated principally within the personal perspective. However, this is only one level in which decisions can be made. In this chapter we have provided three different perspectives, or fields of vision, through which you can navigate your decision-making approach.

As a starting point to any enquiry with a client (whether this is in a one-to-one therapy session, providing feedback to a relative or carer, or participating in discussion about a client's needs in a team meeting), we would recommend that you develop the habit of asking yourself: 'What perspective am I operating within right now – the personal, interpersonal or systemic?' The level at which you are operating will greatly influence your selection of theories, models and methods of intervention. You may not wish to change your Attitude. Nonetheless, by developing a greater awareness of it, you will be clearer about the avenues of enquiry that this will permit and exclude and be better positioned to choose from the decision-making frameworks that we present in this book.

The idea of perspectives, or 'fields of vision', is best regarded as a metaphor for ways of seeing the world, rather than a specific school of thought. As Polkinghorne (1992: 158) remarks, 'The large number of theories claiming to have grasped the essentials of psychological functioning provide prima facie evidence that no one theory is correct'. This has important implications for how we train and practice; if we are imbued with what Farrell (1979) calls 'the ways of talking' of one school it is very difficult to encompass another. Along similar lines, Clarkson (2000) has warned us to be alert to 'schoolism'; that is, passionately held convictions of being right whatever the facts. She challenges us to move beyond schoolism in order to deal more effectively with the multiple realities that impinge on our lives. In thinking about the Attitude that is dominant for you, we recommend that you begin to understand both what your foundational assumptions enable and what they disable in your work.

As O'Neill (2007: 47) comments, 'Seeing with new eyes gives you greater choices when you face the challenges brought to you by your clients'. We hope that this chapter has equipped you with a framework that might uncover some fresh perspectives for engaging with your clients' needs. So your final task is as follows:

- Refer back the Mission statement you previously constructed.
- Consider the perspectives that are most useful for working in that space. Describe these in your learning log.
- Consider what technical and psychological preparation you have undertaken to use these perspectives in the context of your Mission (individual or collective).
- Ask yourself: 'If I were to move towards a different, wider, deeper or more complex perspective, what technical and psychological preparation might be necessary?'
- If these were to be integrated into your service context, what supervisory or support structures would that entail? Are these desirable and feasible?

With this task completed you are now ready to address the ideas in the next chapter: Process.

✍ **Learning summary**

One idea I have found useful in this chapter is. . .

....

....

One thing I would like to experiment with, having read this chapter, is. . .

....

....

Was there anything I didn't quite understand? (If so, I will find out more by. . .)

....

....

Reference

1. When we use the term 'Attitude' we are not referring to a specific psychological construct or psychological theory (we recognize that this term has been used in distinct ways within a range of psychological and therapeutic theories) but rather as a short-hand or metaphoric device to indicate the range of assumptions, beliefs, values – collectively termed 'perspectives' – that therapists and their clients hold about themselves, each other and the aims of therapy. While the term 'Attitude' fits nicely with our 'MAP' mnemonic, in this chapter we use the terms 'Attitude' and 'perspective' interchangeably.

7 Devising a Process for decision-making

> **In this chapter you will learn about:**
> - the range of decision-making tools which you currently use
> - specific strategies for decision-making in different contexts
> - key factors to consider when devising a personalized knowledge-management strategy
>
> **By reading this chapter you will be able to:**
> - reflect on your own Process for making decisions
> - identify which strategies are most likely to work in different decision-making contexts
> - improve your decision-making skills
> - develop a personalized knowledge-management strategy that can improve your decisions with specific clients

Introduction

In the previous chapters you explored your Mission, developed an awareness of your Attitude and considered how these shape your response to your clients' needs. Having done so, you are now ready to consider the final component of MAP – how to design a Process that includes methods of decision-making fit for the Mission you have defined.

The Process element of MAP is perhaps the one that most readily comes to mind when we think about working with a client. It is concerned with the procedures, methods, tools and techniques needed to achieve the contract agreed with the client. Designing a Process involves drawing upon all the resources that you have available – technical and theoretical knowledge, supervisory advice and the available evidence base, as well as an awareness of how both your own and the client's Mission and Attitude shape what is possible. A well-defined Process enables therapists to make effective choices about specific methods of intervention that are needed to achieve particular outcomes.

In this chapter we are concerned with the decision-making Process that makes sense for the Mission you have agreed, and takes account of the parameters imposed by the Attitudes of those involved. This chapter is not, therefore, about all decisions for any situation but rather those you need to hone to work effectively in your context. As a result, as for previous chapters, we would suggest that you focus primarily on those ideas that are relevant to your work setting.

Making decisions in the information era

When trainee therapists are learning how to manage the demands of therapy, or are pursuing a more advanced therapy training at post-qualification level, it is easy to fall into the trap of following the 'rules' of a therapeutic approach without appreciating the thinking that sits behind them.

An example of this occurs fairly frequently for one of us (Sarah) who works with students who have chosen, at post-qualification level, to pursue specialist training in cognitive behaviour therapy. In this way of working, measurement is considered to be very important, with standardized measures frequently used to monitor change. Being highly committed to their clients' development and change, the students typically use such measures very regularly. However, when asked why they have used a particular questionnaire, or how precisely the information obtained will guide their decision-making with a specific client, it is sometimes difficult for students to articulate the reasoning that underpins their choice.

When this occurs, it can be a sign that we have fallen into the trap of following a procedure because we believe we are doing the right thing, rather than because we understand how it might guide us in understanding a client's needs. It is not difficult to appreciate how this can occur in a climate that equates numerical data with credibility and a means to quality control (Wheatley 1999). Moreover, in our culture we consume vast amounts of information. Adair (2010) even makes the point that the *New York Times* contains as much specific information each day as the average person living in the seventeenth century would have accessed in a lifetime! Given these factors, it is easy to confuse following a general guideline (gathering data from questionnaires is a good thing; the more information you have the better) with effective practice (understanding why you have decided to use a particular measure and how you put the information gained to good use). In the information age, it is easy to become sidetracked by the sheer volume of information that we might be able to collect, and to end up confusing quantity with quality.

For this reason, it is essential to have a systematic process for making decisions. This includes having available to you a means of making discriminating judgements about what type of information you need in any particular context, specific decision-making strategies, and a systematic approach to knowledge management (including how you keep your knowledge up to date). The Process component of MAP is concerned with those methods and tools that you need in your armoury of critical thinking skills to support your decision-making in action. Before we look at these further, take some time to review your existing decision-making strategies, using the following exercise.

Exercise 20: *Auditing your range of decision-making tools*

Spend some time thinking about the methods you use when you have to make a decision. Use the questions below to guide you.

- How confident are you that you have useful methods for making successful decisions?
- Are you proactive in your approach to making decisions, or do you prefer to pass the responsibility to others if you can?
- Do you tackle decisions head on, or do you tend to avoid making them if you can?
- How many techniques do you have in your decision-making armoury? Do you tend to use one method or several?
- Do you have a systematic approach to decision-making (i.e. a method or methods you would use in most situations) or do you tend to go along with your 'gut feeling'? If the latter, what do you gain and lose from this?
- How did you learn to make decisions or solve problems in the way that you do? What has shaped your approach?

Also consider whether or not you are satisfied with the range of decision-making tools that you have available to you. Do you feel well equipped to tackle decisions that need to be made at your place of work and in your life generally? Or do you think that this is an area of growth for you? Write down your answers in your learning log and return to them at the end of this chapter to see whether there are any methods that you might now like to try.

Using the four decision quadrants to help you select the right decision-making tool

Having clarified your Mission, and the Attitude associated with this, you will have reached a stage where you are faced with choices. Decisions have to be made about the type of information needed, what weight this information should be given and the most appropriate procedures and methods to use. Typical questions associated with designing a Process include the following:

- In the context of my Mission, and the Attitude I bring to the work, what kind of information do I need to work effectively with this client?
- What methods, tools or procedures are sanctioned and vetoed by my Mission and Attitude? How will this influence my intervention planning?
- What methods, tools or procedures do I need to help guide my decision-making?

In Chapter 5, we identified four quadrants that are relevant to how we define our Mission and which shape our Attitudes. We can use the analogy of the quadrants to consider the decision-making tools needed to guide our work with clients. To recap, the quadrants are illustrated in Figure 3.

Different problem-solving strategies will be required for the different quadrants and, in particular, when we are operating in known (1 and 2) or unknown (3 and 4) quadrants. For example, in quadrants 1 and 2 we can

Quadrant 1. Individual and known	*Quadrant 2. Collective and known*
We are seekers after an individual truth to decide what will work for this client in this context.	We can draw upon a collective understanding of the client's issues; we have an evidence base to enable us to structure our decisions.
Quadrant 4. Individual and unknown	*Quadrant 3. Collective and unknown*
We are faced with an individual journey into the unknown; neither client nor therapist knows what might be appropriate, how to generate change, or if changed is needed.	We are faced with a collective need or competing needs in a social system with no agreed understanding or knowledge base on which to draw; we cannot agree what to do for the best.

Figure 3 The four decision quadrants

draw on structured, linear methods whereby decisions can be based on a step-by-step approach. In contrast, in quadrants 3 and 4 where the decisions may be much more complex, alternative methods will be needed.

The types of decision-making tool that are applicable to working in known and unknown spaces are considered next. As for previous chapters, we would encourage you to consider which quadrant is most applicable to you – and, in particular, whether you are working in the known or unknown spaces – and to focus mainly on the strategies relevant to that space.

How to approach decision-making when your Mission falls in the known quadrants decision-making tools for quadrants 1 and 2

Quadrant 1 (individual and known) is probably most familiar to those working in counselling services and to therapists with an individual caseload. Such services traditionally work from within one of three broad perspectives:

- *Evidence-based.* Therapy is informed by a research literature whereby services are provided from actuarial assessments leading to interventions that 'best fit' the client's needs (such as those best fit interventions for a particular diagnosis or symptom profile).
- *Theoretical.* The service works from a theoretical understanding based in one (occasionally more) field of vision. Client exploration is filtered through a particular worldview which guides both understanding and intervention (e.g. a service specializing in humanistic counselling, a psychodynamic psychotherapy service or a systemic family therapy service).
- *Individualized case formulation.* The service adopts a hypothesis-testing stance in which therapist and client identify and test possible understandings of the predisposing, precipitating and perpetuating factors of influence. The intervention that follows is based upon an individual formulation.

In all three of these stances the enquiry starts with the client's account of their circumstances and then searches for an evidence base to guide the exploration. Thus, the practitioner moves from the particular to the generic and then creates a formulation that satisfies the demand for investigative rigour and individual relevance. Its use assumes that:

- there is an applicable evidence base that can support the enquiry;
- a particular theoretical stance can generate useful insights; or
- a generic hypothesis-testing model could supply appropriate evidence

The types of decisions that are critical here are those relating to *partnership* with the client. The partnership issue is concerned with how the particulars of the client's story can be encompassed within the generic frame that the approach adopts. These two elements, the generic and the particular, are always present (see Lane 1973; Corrie and Lane 2010). For example, in considering someone presenting with features of depression, understanding is required of the commonly cited features of influence on the development and maintenance of depression as well as the evidence base on the effectiveness of different interventions. However, the particular requires that the approach is adapted to take account of the needs of the individual client. Thus, the intervention devised is co-constructed though combining generic and particular stories. In the case of depression, for example, the particular requires that the client is enabled to tell their story in terms of their specific experience of depression. It requires that the client is engaged as a partner in exploring factors which matter to them and others involved.

In *quadrant 2* (collective and known) the types of decisions that will be primary are those concerned with ensuring *coherence*. In this context the aims and objectives of the service are usually clear. The Process used to work with clients is defined in advance of meeting a client in terms of standardized assessment and outcome measures. There may also be a clear protocol for practice or even a manual that you are expected to follow.

Ensuring that such services work well comes down to the extent to which the referral process guides suitable clients into the system, the training provided to staff is adequate, the monitoring of service delivery is consistent and the supervision offered ensures all practitioners adhere to the given framework. Problems occur where staff diverge from the chosen protocol. (On the issue of programme coherence, see, for example, the debates in Lane 1996; and Gosling 2010.)

Where services are highly coherent, with the aims and objectives of the service clearly articulated, it is possible to create effective provision understood by all the relevant parties. Where a service fails in being sufficiently coherent, however, difficulties arise. It may be the case that the therapist delivers an intervention to a client that, while technically appropriate, is rejected as failing to create a sense of coherence with other aspects of their life. Alternatively, for staff, it may be that while there is a clear sense of expectation about what should be delivered, staff fail to embody the sense of the Mission in their day-to-day working lives.

Decision-making in the known quadrants: what methods can I use?

Decisions in the known quadrants tend to lend themselves well to structured decision-making tools and there are some very useful resources available (e.g. Krogerus and Tschäppeler 2008; Adair 2010). Here,

Table 1 A stepped approach to decision-making

Step	Definition	Description
1	Clarify	Clarify the precise nature of the decision that needs to be made. Do not proceed to step 2 until you are confident that you are clear about the question or dilemma to which you need an answer.
2	Generate	Generate as many different options as you can, capitalizing on the capacity of your mind to generate creative and innovative solutions.
3	Evaluate	Now examine the advantages and disadvantages of each option. During step 3 you want to call upon the abilities of the analytical, evaluative mind to consider what you might gain and lose from each option.
4	Short-list	From these options short-list those which you anticipate will be most helpful, most feasible and most acceptable to the key parties involved. Reduce your initial list to about three or four options.
5	Select	Having further evaluated each short-listed option, select the one that you think is the best choice for the decision you need to make.
6	Test	Implement the option and evaluate the results. Is the outcome what you had hoped for? If not, return to step 1 and repeat the process.

decision-making progresses through a distinct series of steps. This introduces a transparency and rigour into the process by requiring us to attend to the mental tasks required at each stage.

Perhaps one of the most commonly used (and powerful) approaches to decision-making is the stepped model, such as that illustrated in Table 1. There are many variations on the stepped approach to decision-making. However, they all share a number of features which are important to remember if you are to use them to good effect.

First, this Process requires an ability to sequence and synthesize the different thinking skills we examined in Part 1. For example, step 1 requires accuracy in thinking – you cannot adequately address a concern unless is it clearly and accurately defined.

Step 2, in contrast, capitalizes on a style of reasoning that entails creativity and innovation in order to generate as many new ideas as possible. A common mistake at step 2 is attempting to evaluate ideas before a sufficient number have been generated. These tasks require different cognitive skills. Generating ideas is a creative mental operation, whereas evaluating the ideas requires analytical mental operations. When you are brainstorming, it is *essential* that you give yourself permission to be as creative as possible *without censoring any of the different options*. Censorship used prematurely restricts creative potential and thus the quality of the decision that is ultimately made. In step 2 it is quantity of ideas that count, not quality.

Step 3 entails the use of skills in analysis and evaluation – here the aim is to reduce the broad range of possibilities into what Adair (2010: 32) describes as a 'diminishing set of feasible options'. The ability to select a particular option and to test out the results of implementing that option against specific predictions relies on accuracy. (We considered some of the different thinking skills needed in Exercise 12 (Chapter 3) when we discussed using de Bono's six thinking hat method – this might be worth revisiting.)

Second, stepped approaches to decision-making assume that you already have (or are capable of acquiring) the information you need to identify the range of options available. This process will not work if you simply do not have the knowledge that is necessary for idea generation. An example here might be if you were attempting to solve a problem in theoretical physics without having any specialist knowledge of this discipline. Equally, in therapy if you are attempting to choose between different methods of intervention, you need knowledge of the range of intervention methods deemed by the therapeutic community to be of potential benefit for the issue at hand. If you do not have the required knowledge, you need to consider whether you are in a position to acquire it or whether it is preferable to refer to someone who does.

Third, stepped approaches also rely on your having clear success criteria. This process is not appropriate if you are unable to determine what a successful outcome would look like. If it is not possible to define the criteria for a good outcome (and this can occur in situations that are highly complex and novel) different decision-making tools are needed.

A further decision-making tool that can be used in the known quadrants is analysis of the potential advantages and disadvantages of a specific course of action. Here, the aim is to identify and then evaluate the pros and cons of a specific course of action. Table 2 provides an illustration of this in relation to a trainee therapist needing to make a decision about whether or not to use imaginal reliving with a client with post-traumatic stress disorder.

If you were supervising this therapist, what would you advise and why? What do you notice about the points listed under each heading that leads you to this recommendation?

One of the benefits of conducting an analysis of the potential advantages and disadvantages of any course of action is that it enables you to take an impartial look at what is pushing you towards, or away from,

Table 2 Exploring the advantages and disadvantages of carrying out reliving with a client with PTSD

Advantages	Disadvantages
The evidence suggests that this is an important intervention to do with clients with PTSD	I have never used this intervention before and feel anxious about doing so
Some of my colleagues have used reliving and it seems to help their clients	The client is using alcohol to manage his difficulties. I suspect that he might have a serious problem with alcohol and I am not sure whether it is safe to carry out reliving in these circumstances
I might speed up my client's progress if I use reliving	I am not yet clear about my formulation – perhaps it's a bit early to start using reliving before I have an understanding of the client's needs
I am keen to learn how to deliver this technique; it will enable me to help more clients effectively in the future	I haven't read enough of the literature on how to conduct reliving to be certain that I could do it properly
There is a pressure in my service to discharge clients as soon as possible to reduce our waiting lists. If I use reliving with this client, I may be able to discharge him sooner and take on someone new	

certain courses of action. It also allows you to identify specific doubts and concerns (as well as gaps in knowledge) that should be taken to supervision.

What we can see from this (fictitious) example is that some points are more compelling than others. For example, avoiding using reliving because the therapist is anxious about using it may not be a valid reasoning for denying the client a potentially effective intervention. A better way of dealing with the anxiety would be to engage in further reading and careful preparation.

However, the absence of a formulation and being unclear about whether reliving is appropriate to carry out while the client is engaged in problem drinking are significant reasons to think more carefully about the best course of action. These 'disadvantages' highlight gaps in knowledge that need to be addressed through further reading, training and supervision. In this case, we could imagine that conducting an analysis of the potential benefits and costs alerted the therapist to the fact that they did not have sufficient knowledge about the circumstances in which to carry out imaginal reliving to proceed with this intervention.

Using a cost–benefit analysis, then, can help you avoid some of the pitfalls of bad decisions by requiring you to be specific about what is guiding your thinking. When using such a method the important questions to ask are the following:

- Have you listed all the potentially relevant factors in each column?
- Which column has the most points in it?
- Which are the most compelling factors identified?
- Are there any factors which, if overlooked, could have serious implications (for you, your client, or others involved)?
- If the advantages and disadvantages listed are considered in terms of short- and long-term benefits and costs, do any new factors emerge?
- Do the anticipated advantages and disadvantages change if the interests of other parties are considered?

When working in the known quadrants, if you have a strong urge to act in a way that is contrary to the logic of your conclusion (based on an analysis of the advantages and disadvantages), this is certainly something that requires further consideration.

Seven useful questions to hold in mind when using a decision-making strategy in the known quadrants are as follows:

1. Do I have all the information I need to make an informed decision? (If not, where can I get it?)
2. Am I clear about the decision that I actually need to make? (Have I spent sufficient time identifying its defining features?)
3. What are the criteria for success in this situation? (How would I know if I made the right decision for this particular situation?)
4. If the decision seems overwhelming, how can I break the question, dilemma or challenge into smaller and more manageable components?
5. Have I clearly identified and thought through all the pros and cons of different potential courses of action – including my favoured option?
6. Do I have the resources (personal, professional, etc.) to implement my chosen strategy?
7. Can I foresee any potential obstacles to the solution I favour that should make me reconsider? (These might be personal, professional, ethical, resource-based, financial – or even legal!)

David's log. Working with Mary

Let us return to the client we first met in Chapter 3 (whom I shall now refer to as Mary). As you will recall, she was referred to the clinical psychology department of the local hospital by her GP, having been given a diagnosis of depression and recommended a course of cognitive behavioural therapy. This was the client whose face dropped when I collected her from the waiting room

The service fitted within quadrant 2 in that there was an agreed process between referral and intervention (the service provided CBT for clients referred for depression). Mary fitted the diagnosis and was open to CBT, which had been explained to her by the GP. There was sufficient information to proceed with an exploration using a CBT process (antecedents, beliefs, consequences) provided that I ignored her expression on meeting me. So there was a lingering issue that I felt needed to be heard.

I asked the question and discovered that she had wanted to see a female therapist. In exploring this I learnt that she had great difficulty with men in general and her husband in particular, and did not believe that a male therapist would be sympathetic to her concerns. I had a choice. I could refer her to a female colleague, or I could continue working with her if she was willing to explore this further. She agreed to continue seeing me as long as a referral to a female therapist remained an option.

Subsequent exploration revealed that her marital relationship had been highly unsatisfactory for many years and that she had stayed only for the children and because she perceived divorce to be a mortal sin. However, there were clear triggers in her husband's behaviour that led to cognitions associated with low mood. The situation was deteriorating as the children had left home. Mary's husband had been out of work for some time and was, therefore, at home more often. In discussing what she wanted from therapy, it was clear that dealing with the depression was not critical. Rather, Mary wanted to find a way to manage her life so that she could remain married but have more 'freedom to be herself'.

Given a complex set of issues, a standardized CBT programme for depression was discarded and so the move was made from quadrant 2 to quadrant 1. (Within my team, this was an allowed process.) An individualized case formulation was adopted; that is, a series of hypotheses about the issues that concerned her were jointly constructed and tested in a set of experiments with behaviour. Eventually a programme was agreed that included ways to manage her relationship with her husband, her children, her colleagues (who also were problematic) and her relationship with herself. Six months of weekly therapy resulted in the depression becoming well managed and her gaining space to do the things she wanted, without her husband, while remaining married. One year later, a follow-up appointment revealed that she was much happier with her life at home and at work.

How would this case have been handled in your setting? What decision process might you have used?

How to approach decision-making when your Mission falls in the unknown quadrants: decision-making tools for quadrants 3 and 4

The decision-making tools that apply in the known quadrants are based on the assumption that the decision to be made or the problem to be solved is (with a little effort) relatively easily defined and largely uncontentious – in other words, that those with knowledge of a given area would agree on the nature of the problem or decision. However, this is not necessarily the case when we are operating in the unknown quadrants. If these quadrants apply to you, then the following section offers some ideas for how to navigate this terrain. If not, you may wish to go straight to the conclusion of this chapter.

In *quadrant 3* (collective and unknown) we are faced with having to make decisions under conditions of uncertainty where it is not possible to predict that any particular outcome will occur.

In quadrant 3 the Process that is often most helpful is one of tracking decision-making over time and finding ways to understand and modify those decisions as the work unfolds. This approach has value where group members, although differing in their views, are nonetheless prepared to undertake an experiment on their own behaviour by tracking the decision-making process they habitually use, observing the results obtained and making changes in light of those results. Here, the experiments undertaken do not aim to discover a linear truth (there is no simplistic cause–effect relationship or right or wrong answer) but rather to explore and better understand the process the group members are going through. Essentially, people meet to define the decision they need to make but agree to explore their own process in order to create a more effective procedure for decision-making. This approach might progress through a four-stage analysis as follows:

1. The group agrees to track how individual members structure their decisions in the group. Members are encouraged to be interested

not just in their own decisions but also the process of making them. In particular, they need to track the relative priority given to different elements of the situation and how and what they pay attention to over time. The 'over time' part is particularly important as it aids an ability to examine the process reflectively.

2. As the group reaches decision points, they explore which parts of the process of arriving at the decision felt consistent with their individual core values and any that violated their basic values. The next stage involves the group searching for elements of the process which support shared values in order to create a prototype for moving forward.

3. As these prototypes emerge, the group observes how they feel about the choices they make in comparison with the previous process used. Did it feel better at the time and subsequently? This enables the group to retain an intuitive awareness of what resonates with them.

4. Once they have a prototype which is right for the group, members deliberately use this to structure their decision-making. They voice the shared expectations they have of each other in making a decision and also the shared values that underpin the process. Members then agree the standards (norms) which will guide the decisions they make, including finding a way within their prototype of choosing to act on matters that are within their control and mitigating the effects of those outside their control.

David's log. Decision-making around strategy in a science services company

A group of managers and researchers in a science services company were struggling with decision-making around strategy in view of significant changes in the market sector they served. The service that they had traditionally provided was being undermined by the advent of high-powered internet searching and increasingly specialized software. The problem was not simply finding a new strategy but the way they made decisions (team members used their intellect to argue for their own favoured decision and sought to undermine the arguments of others). Where a decision could not be reached the senior management team imposed one which everyone needed to adopt (even if, privately, individuals disagreed).

I had been asked to offer a mediation to help the teams consider how they made decisions. In approaching me, it appeared that they had already taken a step in the direction of a willingness to consider their current decision-making practices.

So what actually happened? A number of models exist for understanding and assisting team decision-making (we examine this literature in Chapter 9). In consequence, if the team had been willing to adopt one of these structured decision models from the literature, they could have developed a different approach (i.e. we could have designed a solution by operating within quadrant 2). However, from initial conversations it was clear that they rejected any decision-making tool designed elsewhere on the basis that 'it would not work here'. Further discussion revealed that the team was still focused on outcomes rather than on developing a process for understanding how they were arriving at a decision. There were conflicting ideas on what that outcome should be (in other words, conflict over how the Mission should be defined).

In considering this they were able to agree that the present decision process was unsatisfactory but felt, given their knowledge, that they should be able to find a way to improve it. They agreed to use the four-stage analysis process outlined above in which they tracked the decisions made over time. They examined each of the areas by asking questions to try to understand how they arrived at decisions. From the understanding derived from engaging with these questions, it became possible to identify what a prototype for a new framework might look like. That framework included a clear Mission statement, an understanding of the perspectives (Attitude) they needed to bring to future decision-making and an agreed Process for decision-making based on the prototype they developed. Rather than a model being imposed from outside, this process gave them a self-developed framework that they felt 'would work here'.

A decision-making approach such as this enables a team, department or service to build its own decision process which they can use in the uncertain situations they face. In the collective and unknown quadrant the primary issue is one of *dialogue* and enabling decision-making that is different, wider, deeper and more complex.

Quadrant 4 (individual and unknown) is a very challenging place to work and requires considerable psychological preparation of self for the role (in Stanislavski's terms). It is a place which, if encountered early in a career, needs to be taken directly to supervision and easily taps into the decision biases described in Chapter 1. The practitioner needs to be well prepared in terms of their own awareness of self and practised in the ability to recognize when they are fully present with the client. The primary process issue here is one of *presence*.

There are elements here that will feel familiar, if complicated. It is a place in which the practitioner works entirely from the client's frame of reference, using the client's story as the basis for enquiry and discovery. Thus, the decision-making approaches that operate in the known quadrants (stepped approach, analysis of pros and cons, etc.) become less applicable. The emphasis in the first instance is on capturing the lived experience of individuals in terms of their own approach to meaning making, grounded in the belief that individuals construct their experiences through drawing on implicit theories about self, other and the world. Theoretical models which focus on the client's lived experience can provide a starting point, but the practitioner has to be very aware that reliance on those models could result in missing the essence of the dilemma.

We are operating in this space when our implicit theories no longer make sense. There are no protocols, therapeutic models or evidence base fitting the nature of the work in hand and so there is a lack of substantive guidance on when and how to act that could lead both therapist and client to feel less anxious. As we discussed in Chapter 3, this is about staying with the tension and using the anxiety as a source of creativity. In part we are engaged in an endeavour that has overlap with qualitative research methods where the aim is to create what Josselson and Lieblich (2003: 259) describe as an 'interpreted description of the rich and multilayered meanings of historical and personal events'.

This does not mean that there is nothing in our professional armoury to offer the client, but rather that we have to be prepared to engage with what emerges and stay with this material even if this evokes anxiety. There are questions that are helpful in this space to begin to explore the lived experience and the implicit theories that guide it. The key, however, is to stay alert to the emergent properties in the conversation.

David's log. A child with problematic behaviour

Relatively early in my career I was asked to work with an 8-year-old child who was in constant trouble for hitting, bumping and generally annoying other children in class.

The teacher had been asked to undertake some baseline measurements of the occurrence of the behaviours in class. As these were sufficiently frequent to observe I also had the opportunity to sit in class and try to record the antecedent–behaviour–consequence pattern that occurred for each event. This proved difficult as no discernible pattern emerged. A look at the child's records indicated some mild learning difficulties. Recent incidents of the child wetting himself in class had also been recorded. The child had difficulty with some physical activities and appeared quite clumsy. Further investigation of this was needed so parental permission was sought. The parents wanted me to visit them at home before they would agree. They explained that the child had started wetting the bed and also had broken a number of items in the house. Asked how they dealt with this, they said they punished him as the Bible required – spare the rod and spoil the child. They did, however, agree to further investigation.

Following some neurological testing the child was found to have some difficulties with spatial awareness that meant he had difficulty locating himself in space without touching objects around him. Looking back at the class observations, they could now be understood as the child hitting and bumping to find his way around. Analysis of his wetting indicated it was generated by anxiety about possible punishment at home and school.

So we now had a clear formulation and were potentially in quadrant 1. In discussing this with the parents, however, they rejected this explanation and stated their determination to punish the child for wilfulness (this time showing me the rod they used) as this was God's Word. In the context of this case, it is important to recognize that at this time teachers still used to cane children as punishment and within some church schools this was also a common event.

So I was in unknown territory – but so were the parents, who were coping with a child whose behaviour seemed inexplicable except as wilfulness that needed to be punished. Similarly, the child's teacher was in unknown territory trying to cope with a child whose behaviour was disruptive to the class (and therefore should be punished) and resented by other children. However, the teacher had not identified an effective way to respond either. The formulation, however elegant, was not accepted by all key parties and therefore any intervention was problematic.

So where might I now go with this? What decision process might I use? As my supervisor, how might you have advised me?

Decision–making in the unknown quadrants: what methods can I use?

Working in the unknown quadrants can be highly challenging as they do not lend themselves well to structured decision-making techniques. This is for two principal reasons:

1. It is typically difficult to agree on objectives. There are often multiple and competing expectations in operation, with different individuals holding very different beliefs about the best way to proceed.
2. It is difficult to predict the outcomes of any action taken. There is no straightforward relationship between cause and effect.

Recent developments in a number of fields can support us in making decisions in the unknown quadrants. Cavanagh and Lane (2012), for example, propose that practitioners need to become increasingly well-versed in thinking about the world as a 'messy system'.

The types of decisions we face when operating in the unknown quadrants may, therefore, be of a qualitatively different kind than those typical of simple systems. Kahane (2007) suggests that in complex systems the types of challenge we face are:

- dynamically complex (cause and effect are only distantly related in space and time, which makes them difficult to understand);
- generatively complex (they unfold in ways that are unfamiliar and unpredictable);
- socially complex (the various stakeholders can see the situation in very different ways, which tends to result in views becoming polarized and progress prevented).

As a consequence we cannot make successful decisions by seeking straightforward cause–effect relationships, using a stepped approach to decision-making or reviewing the benefits and costs. We have to develop ways of approaching decision-making that enable us to appreciate and work productively with the fact that each of the parties will have different, possibly contradictory but equally legitimate views. Thus, the approach is not about finding the true or accurate account, but a workable account that enables us to go forward. For example, in the case of the child with problematic behaviour, one of the key issues was how to develop a dialogue between the different stakeholders (who had very different expectations) without becoming polarized.

In such circumstances, dialogue is a very powerful decision-making tool. Dialogue is different from discussion or disputation. In discussion and disputation each party tries to present their argument by gathering data and canvassing opinion to support it and contesting the alternatives. Where they persist in trying to prove they are right and the other wrong we have a disputation process. However, in complex space the likelihood is that no one can be right. Dialogue, in contrast, is where different parties explore together. Recognizing that no one can know the right answer, it becomes possible to engage in a reflective dialogue which enables each party to sense intuitively the way forward to potential understandings that might be shared. Out of this they can create generative dialogue which transcends individual understanding and creates new ways of seeing. These subsequently enable solutions to emerge. Dialogue occurs where the parties involved seek to find common ground and achieve a bigger perspective that is capable of incorporating all parties' views.

Generative dialogue requires a willingness to think carefully about who might need to be included. This may involve being prepared to 'widen the circle', in Kahane's terms, by including those whose perspectives are uncomfortable to hear and whose experiences, whilst relevant to the discussion, do not constitute socially sanctioned accounts of what is and is not permitted.

When working in the unknown quadrants it is important to spend time looking at how the Process unfolds and what emerges for you and the client or clients (you may often find yourself working with a system or systems rather than an individual when working in the unknown quadrants). On the basis of this understanding you can identify decision models that could be useful to you in the future. It is very helpful to think about the story that emerges and explore the following:

- How did different aspects of the story connect with each other to make sense of the presenting concern? What was left in and left out, with what implications for the thread of the story? How did that change over time within the conversation? The issue of noticing over time is central to working in this space – what Corrie and Lane (2010) term the 'narrative structure'.
- What was the degree of richness of the story and how was the explanatory account put together? Who contributed information/ideas to its development? How were ideas incorporated and discarded? How rich was the story, as revealed by its quality, style and complexity? How did that change over time within the conversation (the narrative process)?

- What was the content of the story? The 'what' consists of information at the level of data (client's and practitioner's), theory, models developed by others and research. What theories of causation did the participants propose to explain the predicament and how did the process of identifying a possible new story emerge? How did that change over time within the conversation (the narrative content)?

Exploration of the themes and connecting to the felt sense they contain for both client and therapist taps into the intuitive understanding. So you pay attention to what is happening inside and outside over time. As we saw in Chapter 3, this is a possible way of going deeper into the client experience. As a practitioner thinking about decision processes to use in this quadrant, it is important to recognize that we are not looking for empirical (factual) truth but rather a sense of truthfulness for yourself and the client. The tools do not look like the propositional/paradiagmatic frameworks with which psychology is replete. This mode of enquiry does not aim to identify themes that are generalizable in the empirical sense. In terms of Process, we are looking at the story though a different and wider lens but primarily we are looking to go deeper into ourselves and with our clients.

When working in the unknown quadrants, useful questions to hold in mind when selecting and implementing a decision-making strategy include the following:

- Whose stories need to be heard?
- How can I act as a good facilitator of others' stories?
- How do different aspects of the stories connect with each other?
- Do those connections help us make sense of the present concern?
- What is left in and left out?
- Who contributed information/ideas to its development?
- How were ideas incorporated and discarded?
- What elements in the stories help us explain the predicament?
- How can I enhance the possibility of us working together to identify a new shared story that has implications for moving forward?

Developing an effective approach to knowledge management

Regardless of whether you work primarily in the known or unknown quadrants, it is important to consider what type of knowledge you will need in order to work effectively as a therapist and how you can keep your knowledge up to date. Successful decision-making depends, in part, upon having access to the information that you need, but, as we noted at the start of this chapter, the amount of information is increasing at an exponential rate. It is not possible to be aware of all the information that is being produced, and even if it were, not all of it is accurate. As a result, you will need a strategy for discriminating between information that is credible and that which is misleading or frankly bogus, and for selecting sources of knowledge that will enable you to keep yourself up to date in the areas that are critical to providing an effective service to your clients. There are a number of steps that you can take to enhance your knowledge-management approach:

- Carry out a regular appraisal or audit of your knowledge to identify areas of strength and gaps. Get into the habit of setting goals for yourself in terms of enhancing your understanding of areas that are relevant to your practice.
- Make sure that you also regularly audit your thinking skills. Spend some time reflecting on decisions that were more and less effective and see what you can learn. Are there specific situations where your skills tend to fail you?
- As part of your professional development, create some protected time for reading. It is impossible to read everything that may be relevant, so plan in advance which journals (academic and trade), books and databases contain the type of information that is most relevant to your practice and access these regularly. In addition:
  - wherever possible, obtain original articles rather than relying on secondary sources:
  - get in the habit of deliberately reading articles where the author holds a view that is different from your own. This can test your skills in critical thinking in a helpful way.
- Ensure that you can access relevant databases and important research studies. Keep informed about broader debates in the therapy professions concerning best practice
- Develop a network of colleagues who have a particular interest in related, but different, fields from your own. Use this network as a means of sharing information.
- Remember to consider your critical thinking skills, as distinct from your discipline-specific knowledge. Invest in your critical thinking skills by looking for opportunities to exercise these regularly (using the exercises in this book will help you in this).

Exercise 21: *Pulling it all together*

Having completed the tasks on decision process you will now need to pull together the learning from the Mission, Attitude and Process chapters to create a MAP for decision-making that makes sense of the context (quadrant) in which you operate. Write down each element of your MAP, read it out loud and ensure that it resonates. If it does not, go back and rework it, and check for resonance until it intuitively feels right. Then assess it reflectively. Does it help you to negotiate decision-making in your work with clients in your context? When it does, the work of this chapter is done.

Conclusion

There are many different decision-making tools available that can support you in designing a more efficient and effective Process for working with your clients. However, your ability to select and implement these different tools will be more effective if you are able to match the technique to the quadrant in which you are working.

In this chapter, we have proposed that the known and unknown quadrants require different decision-making strategies. The former lend themselves particularly well to structured, linear approaches. In the known quadrants, cause–effect relationships are relatively straightforward in the sense that the decision that needs to be made can be relatively easily defined, a range of potential solutions can be generated and then a selected decision can be tested for effectiveness. This does not, of course, mean that decision-making is easy! As we saw in Chapter 1, decision-making biases highlight the ease with which this process can go astray. Nonetheless, if we adopt a disciplined approach the tools available will enhance our potential for successful decision-making in the known quadrants.

In contrast, when operating in the unknown quadrants where the decision to be made is difficult to define, where cause–effect relationships are unclear and the outcome is likely to reflect the influence of multiple factors that we can neither predict nor control, relying on our individual mental operations is insufficient. We need to look beyond simple strategies and formulae to embrace methods of decision-making that are grounded in listening, dialogue and an exchange of ideas and values grounded in mutual respect and a willingness to listen.

We started this chapter by suggesting that you would be able to:

- reflect on your own Process for making decisions;
- identify which strategies are most likely to work in different decision-making contexts;
- improve your decision-making skills;
- develop a personalized knowledge-management strategy that can improve your decisions with specific clients.

Hopefully you now feel able to create your own Process that enables different decision models of value to you and your clients in the context in which you operate.

✍ Learning summary

One idea I have found useful in this chapter is. . .

....

....

One thing I would like to experiment with, having read this chapter, is. . .

....

....

Was there anything I didn't quite understand? (If so, I will find out more by. . .)

....

....

Part III

Decision-making contexts that require special consideration

Having completed the chapters in Part 2, you now have your MAP – a systematic approach to making, evaluating and refining your therapist decisions that is fit for purpose in your work setting (and possibly beyond!). We would encourage you to use this regularly to ensure that you can capitalize on the evidence base of your discipline, state-of-the-art developments, and the wisdom of your own experience as your career progresses.

Before we conclude this book, we turn our attention to two decision-making contexts that require special consideration because of their unique characteristics, functions and demands on the therapist: first, supervision; and second, working in teams. These chapters build upon the frameworks previously discussed and rely on some of the exercises you will have already completed. For these reasons, Chapters 8 and 9 are best read once you have developed your decision MAP as recommended in Chapter 5.

In Chapter 10, we conclude the book with some final comments about decision-making as a basis for planning the next stage of your career as a professional decision-maker. We offer you a reflective tool as an aid to pulling together the core ideas contained in the previous chapters. We hope that you will want to return to this tool again and again as a method for helping you reflect upon, and continuously improve, your decision-making capability.

We acknowledge that we live and work in unprecedented times and that the types of decisions we are required to make as professionals are increasingly complex. We believe that the tools we have described throughout the book and reprised here will continue to be helpful to you throughout your career.

8   Decision-making in supervision

In this chapter you will learn about:

- the multiple functions of supervision
- some of the factors that may help and hinder best use of supervision
- how you can use the MAP model to get the most out of supervision

By reading this chapter you will be able to:

- know what questions to ask your supervisor at the start of your working relationship
- capitalize on the learning opportunities provided in supervision
- monitor the progress in your knowledge, skills and developmental process

---

Introduction

Over the course of our careers much of our decision-making will be supported by, and scrutinized within, supervision. For most schools of therapy and the professional bodies that accredit them, supervision is deemed to be an essential component of therapist development. It is also recognized by policy-makers as having a vital role to play in enhancing the quality of practice (see Department of Health 2004). As a result, we can expect to stay in supervision for the duration of our working lives, although its function and form may vary as a result of our individual training needs, career stage and service context.

As one of the primary vehicles through which professional development takes place, supervision can be seen as a decision-making context in its own right – a learning environment that enables us to reflect upon, analyse and evaluate decisions that we make with and about our clients, and to consider the implications of these decisions for forward planning.

This chapter helps you to think about how to make good use of supervision in order to enhance your practice as a professional decision-maker. Using MAP, we provide a framework that can enable you to capitalize on the learning opportunities on offer, as well as navigate any tensions that might arise.

Before we begin, spend some time thinking about your experiences of supervision so far, using the following exercise to guide you.

Exercise 22:   *Auditing your experiences of supervision*

Identify a positive experience of supervision that you have had. Recall the context in which it took place (the service setting, whether an individual or group format was adopted, etc.), the defining features (e.g. your supervisor's interpersonal style, the roles he or she adopted and any specific procedures or techniques used) and what qualities were present and absent. Based on your recollection of this, can you identify which factors helped make this a positive experience? What types of guidance and support were you given and how did they impact on your decision-making with clients?

Now identify a less positive, or even downright negative, experience of supervision (if you have had any!). Recall the context in which it took place (the service setting, whether an individual or group format was adopted, etc.); the defining features (e.g. your supervisor's interpersonal style, the roles he or she adopted and any specific procedures or techniques used) and what qualities were present and absent. Based on your recollection of this, can you identify what factors contributed to this being a negative experience? What types of guidance and support were you given and how did this impact on your decision-making with clients?

What might these experiences tell you about your own needs in supervision and what works most and least effectively for you? Considering both examples, can you make any links back to ideas we discussed in the previous chapters? Keep your answers in mind as you work through the remainder of this chapter.

Learning in supervision

Of all the vehicles for developing professional competence, supervision is arguably the most critical. As an integral component of learning how to be a therapist, it would be both irregular and unethical if you were to progress through your training without the support of at least one supervisor who has responsibility for helping you reflect on and evaluate your work with clients.

Supervision provides 'a formal, independent process of reflection and review which enables practitioners to increase individual self-awareness, develop their competence and critique their work' (Lane and Corrie 2006: 192). As such, it is widely regarded as an important form of continuing professional development. Indeed, supervision is enshrined within the formal guidelines of many professional bodies, such as the British Psychological Society (2006) and the British Association for Counselling and Psychotherapy's Code of Ethics (2010). It is also central to the UK government initiative, *Improving Access to Psychological Therapies* (IAPT; Department of Health 2008), whereby the drive to increase access to empirically supported interventions has resulted in a demand for high-quality CBT-focused supervision that can support therapist development, ensure adherence to procedure and enhance treatment effectiveness.

The importance afforded supervision by our professional and regulatory bodies would appear to be echoed by supervisors and supervisees, who tend to rate this learning context highly (Lucock et al. 2006). Nonetheless, despite generally high levels of endorsement, supervision is not without its challenges. Indeed, Liese and Beck (1997) note that supervision can prove just as complex as therapy to conduct effectively.

Negative experiences of supervision do occur and can have a destructive impact on both the supervision process and supervisee development (Ramos-Sánchez et al. 2002). In the same way that clients report finding some therapists or types of therapy more helpful than others, so we are likely to experience some supervisors as being more or less productive.

Our experiences (both positive and negative) are likely to reflect a range of factors, including whether there is a good match between the supervisor and supervisee's interpersonal styles and the effectiveness of the supervisory methods used. However, they are also likely to reflect the inherent complexity of the task itself. As Wampold and Holloway (1997) observe, supervision is a professional activity that is difficult to conceptualize and operationalize, partly because its instructional and supportive elements exist alongside monitoring and evaluative components. A similar point has been made by Lane (2011), who observes that while there is little debate that supervision is a valuable context for learning, there is less agreement about what exactly constitutes 'supervision', whether it can be precisely defined, and whether it is necessary throughout a career or just while training.

Supervision also overlaps with other elements of professional training and practice such as formal teaching, self-directed learning and personal therapy, rendering its distinct contribution difficult to isolate and measure. Perhaps for these reasons, there have been few high-quality systematic reviews, few studies that examine directly how client change and therapist performance are related to supervision, and currently no substantive evidence-based guidelines on what best practice in supervision might actually entail (Milne 2009). Although the training and accreditation of supervisors is attracting increased professional interest, and despite attempts to specify the competences required to deliver CBT-focused supervision (Roth and Pilling 2007), there are still relatively few formal training opportunities that offer a systematic approach to developing the knowledge and skills necessary to become a good supervisor. Supervision, it seems, is an emerging discipline. Nevertheless, much is happening. The British Psychological Society (2006, 2011) has spent five years looking at supervision before adopting a set of competences for supervision. Additionally, the British Association for Counselling and Psychotherapy has a long-established accreditation process for supervision.

Where does this leave you as the supervisee? In his study of the relationship between supervisors and supervisees, Carroll (1996: 92) found that supervisees tend to 'have few expectations from which to negotiate with supervisors, and are prepared to "fall in" with the supervisor's ways of setting up and engaging in supervision'. As a result, when meeting a supervisor for the first time, you will probably have many questions (and anxieties!) about how this new relationship might develop. Typical questions might include the following:

- Will my supervisor like and understand me?
- Will they be able to meet my needs for learning and support?
- Can I be honest about my practice with this person?
- How am I going to get the most out of supervision?
- What are my supervisor's expectations of me?
- How will my supervisor evaluate my competence and what implications will this have?

If it is to fulfil its potential as a transformational learning environment, supervision needs careful thought and preparation. Both supervisor and supervisee need to be clear about its purpose (Mission) and the perspectives (Attitude) about supervision and therapy practice that will guide the learning agreement. There also needs to be a consensus about the procedures and techniques (Process) that will be used and by which the purpose will be realized. In short, in order to get the most out of supervision, you need a MAP.

Developing a MAP for supervision

As you will recall (and if you cannot, now would be a good time to refer back to Chapter 4), the MAP model emphasizes the need to develop a clear understanding of the fundamental purpose of the activity you are about to undertake (Mission), the factors that influence the expectations of the different parties involved, including preferred therapeutic models and beliefs about therapy (Attitude), and the procedures, methods and techniques needed to meet the learning objectives specified in the contract (Process).

MAP can help you organize some of the decisions that you need to make which are central to establishing productive supervisory relationships. These include negotiating a contract, developing an awareness of the perspectives that underpin your own and your supervisor's approach (including areas of similarity and difference) and being clear about the type of supervisory methods that may be used. You can also use MAP as a framework for navigating questions about, and tensions that can occur within, supervision should they arise. So let us look at this in more detail.

Mission

As we suggested earlier in this chapter, the purpose and form of the supervision we receive is likely to vary as a result of our individual training needs, career stage and service context. Lane (2011) describes this in terms of supervision occupying 'different professional spaces'. For example, its traditional role has been interpreted as apprenticeship, where a student learns their craft from a more experienced practitioner. When you start out in your career, and especially when you are undergoing formal training, this is the implicit interpretation of supervision that is likely to inform how you and your supervisor define your work together. However, as we become more experienced, supervision tends to become a field of activity between experienced practitioners. Here, when we have some confidence in our therapeutic knowledge and skills, we find ourselves defining the purpose of supervision differently as a function of having multiple roles and needing approaches to learning and support that are relevant to our area of expertise.

The idea that supervision occupies different professional spaces in diverse contexts goes some way towards understanding the complexity of the endeavour. As Milne et al. (2009) observe, one of the challenges facing supervisors and supervisees is that their work together typically has to fulfil a range of functions. These functions and the relative focus given to each will vary according to the professional space in which it is provided. For this reason, we need to be clear about the purpose of any supervisory engagement in order to capitalize on the learning experience that is on offer.

Let us examine the different types of Mission that might be implicit in some common working definitions of supervision. Consider, for example, one of the most widely cited definitions (Bernard and Goodyear 2004: 8) in which supervision is:

> an intervention provided by a more senior member of a profession to a more junior member or members of that same profession. This relationship is evaluative, extends over time, and has the simultaneous purposes of enhancing the professional function for the more junior person(s), monitoring the quality of professional services offered to the clients she, he, or they see, and serving as a gatekeeper for those who are to enter the particular profession.

Here, we see references to the evaluative and quality control components of supervision, with the emphasis on supervision being provided by more senior practitioners to more junior staff members (the apprenticeship model).

Milne (2009: 15) equally emphasizes the evaluative component but gives additional priority to the educational, supportive and developmental aspects. Here supervision is defined as:

> the formal provision, by approved supervisors, of a relationship-based education and training that is work-focused and which manages, supports, develops and evaluates the work of colleague/s ... It therefore differs from related activities, such as mentoring and therapy, by incorporating an evaluative component ... and by being obligatory. The main methods that supervisors use are corrective feedback on the supervisees' performance, teaching, and collaborative goal-setting.

The definition provided by the Department of Health (2003: 3) includes features of both learning and support but also frames these in the context of client safety:

> [supervision is] ... a formal process of professional support and learning which enables individual practitioners to develop knowledge and competence, assume responsibility for their own practice and enhance consumer protection and safety of care in complex clinical situations.

Given the complexity of supervision, it is perhaps unsurprising that a number of definitions exist. Nonetheless, on closer examination we can

see that, following Proctor (1986) – see http://www.emccouncil.org/src/
ultimo/models/Download/7.pdf – these definitions share a number of features relating to the following functions:

1. The *normative* function – that is, where supervision adopts a managerial role, ensuring that supervisees are following relevant organizational procedures, operating within professional guidelines and working safely with clients.
2. The *formative* function – that is, where supervisors operate as teachers, instructors or coaches, assessing level of knowledge and skill in order to provide information and guidance on specific therapeutic activities and tasks.
3. The *restorative* function – that is, where supervisors offer support, provide containment and create an environment of safety and trust in which the dilemmas encountered in therapy can be openly discussed.

There are a number of other functions that supervision can serve. For example, Holloway (1997) includes enhancing self-awareness and the ability for self-evaluation as part of a broader approach to professional role development. Additionally, depending on the stage of career development, supervision might serve a more consultative function, whereby supervisees share responsibility for and take active ownership of their development.

Of all the different functions that supervision serves, it is perhaps the evaluative aspect of supervision that is the most anxiety-provoking. As part of a broader quality control agenda, supervisors are generally expected to assess the competence of their supervisees. This can take numerous forms. For example, it might entail the supervisor providing feedback on specific skills or areas of practice. Or it might be an ongoing process as part of a training contract where the supervisor gradually builds up a picture of the supervisee's competence in order to reach a decision about whether to pass a student at the end of the placement. Alternatively, it might take the form of a graded piece of work. One example of this would be the supervisor rating a therapy session on a specific measure of competence, such as the Cognitive Therapy Scale – Revised (Blackburn et al. 2001) commonly used in CBT practice. Additionally, supervisors act as gatekeepers for their professions, and thus for society, with the authority to determine whether supervisees meet the criteria for standards demanded by relevant credentialing bodies.

In relation to the evaluative component of supervision, issues of hierarchy and power become particularly apparent. In their work in this area, Murphy and Wright (2005) note that the issue of power in supervision has been poorly represented in the literature and that supervisees' perspectives have largely been absent from the debate. This would seem to be a significant oversight, given the essentially hierarchical nature of most supervisory relationships and the fact that power differences have been noted to impact significantly on these professional relationships and even on therapeutic outcomes (Nelson and Friedlander 2001).

Abuses of power can result in harm to clients in a number of ways. Supervisees may feel unable to reveal information about their work with clients for fear of a supervisor abusing boundaries (Emerson 1996) such as forcing self-disclosure, straying into providing therapy or even engaging in sexually inappropriate behaviour (Bonosky 1995). Other abuses of power and hierarchy noted include verbally undermining supervisees, overburdening them with too many cases and forcing them to adhere to supervisors' own theoretical frameworks (Porter and Vasquez 1997).

Although the emphasis in the literature has been on supervisors' power, it has been observed that supervisees also have power and can use this unethically through, for example, withholding information, providing unwarranted critical evaluations of their supervisors or making false allegations against them (Ladany 2004). Power and the ethical management thereof must, therefore, be seen as a shared responsibility, even though the hierarchical positions of supervisor and supervisee are unequal.

Of course, hierarchy and power are not necessarily bad. As Murphy and Wright (2005) emphasize, when used ethically they can, particularly early in our careers, provide a sense of safety and containment. Equally, they note that supervisors can use their power productively to increase supervisees' awareness of interpersonal dynamics (Cohen 1998) and model ways in which hierarchy can foster trust (Kaiser 1992).

How issues of hierarchy and power are understood, and how any ethical dilemmas arising will be managed, will be context-dependent. As noted by McCann (2011), supervision during training reflects the coming together of at least three distinct systems: the training institution, the supervisor and supervisee, and the organization or agency in which the service to clients is provided. The way in which the relationship between these three systems is managed is critical to the supervisee's experience of supervision. We propose that it is also essential to consider other stakeholders who might exert an influence on the way in which supervision is delivered. For example, in the context of the IAPT initiative described earlier, the funding provided to services is contingent upon providing a national team with data on clinical outcomes. Services as well as individual therapists are being scrutinized as to whether they are meeting required targets. This impacts on how the supervisory Mission is defined, which in turn determines how supervision is actually delivered.

Exercise 23:   *Towards developing a shared supervisory Mission*

How do you imagine your supervisor would define supervision? Knowing this will give you invaluable insight into the Mission that guides the approach taken, including the relative weight given to the different functions outlined previously. You might like to organize your dialogue with your supervisor using the following questions:

- What is the context in which you are both working together? Who or what has had a role in shaping this?
- What is your supervisor's purpose in supervision? What are they setting out to achieve? How does this relate to your own purpose? Do you have a match or mismatch?
- Can you agree a clearly stated, negotiated purpose to supervision? If so, what is it? What are you both setting out to achieve?
- How will you both recognize and manage the power differential and any challenges arising from it?

Attitude

As applied to supervision, the Attitude component of MAP is concerned with trying to understand those factors that influence both parties' expectations of each other and of the supervisory process. This includes expectations about the balance between the different functions of supervision, the extent to which supervision is seen as task-focused or developmentally oriented, and beliefs about the learning processes through which therapists increase their knowledge and skill.

Watkins (1997) proposes that there are a number of factors that influence how supervisors work (and we would add that these factors are equally relevant to how the supervisee approaches supervision). These are: (1) the assumptive world; (2) the theory or model used; (3) supervisory style; (4) roles and strategies; (5) foci; (6) format of supervision; and (7) technique. For the purposes of Attitude, it is the first three factors identified by Watkins that require particular attention.

The notion of the assumptive world refers to factors that encompass life experience, professional experience and personal values as well as our schema about therapy, our clients, and what it means to be a therapist. This rich tapestry of experiences, values and beliefs frames the theory or model that is dominant in any supervisor's (and supervisee's) thinking and approach.

As we saw in Chapter 6, each therapeutic approach has a unique perspective on human experience and advocates a particular route to change. The therapeutic approaches to which you and your supervisor adhere will impact critically on what is discussed as well as the style of delivery that supervision takes. This will afford both benefits and challenges. Knowing the theoretical model that guides your supervisor's outlook will result in greater clarity about what to expect, but our theoretical vocabularies, so easily mistaken for certainty, can prevent us from remaining attuned to the client's story (Anderson and Swim 1995). No matter how careful we are in our use of terminology, or how sensitive to our clients' individual circumstances, our perspectives both enable and constrain us in our ability to work effectively with clients. This can equally be said of supervision where, with the client physically absent, the perspectives of both supervisor and supervisee will dominate decision-making in ways that the client might not necessarily endorse.

A further critical factor is the supervisor's theory of supervision. Different models of supervision operate from different assumptive worldviews. For example, Anderson and Swim (1995: 1) define supervision as a 'collaborative conversation that is generative and relational, through which supervisees create their own answers, and in doing so experience freedom and self-competence'. Underpinned by a post-modern perspective, knowledge and learning are understood as socially constructed through discourse. The assumptive worldview is that supervisees retain the expertise on their own lives, narratives and knowledge. This in turn is reflected in the aim of supervision, which is seen as providing a context for co-creation of new meaning that affords the potential for change.

Contrast this perspective with a therapist who is providing a manualized form of therapy for a particular mental health problem (such as depression) as part of a research trial. Here, supervision will be organized around delivering a specified intervention with a high degree of technical skill. The supervisor retains the role of expert in guiding the therapist and shaping practice. The assumptive worldview is that optimum therapeutic effectiveness (in terms of therapy outcome) is achieved through close adherence to the manualized intervention, usually supported by empirical evidence. Ensuring adherence to the model will, therefore, be a central focus in supervision and will determine the supervisory methods used, which are likely to include formal ratings of audio- or video-recorded therapy sessions.

Milne (2009) has developed a helpful classification that can enable us to navigate our way through different approaches to supervision. As at least one of these is likely to influence your supervisor's approach, it can provide a basis for discussion at the start of any new supervisory relationship. Milne's classification is as follows:

- developmental models – derived from lifespan development theory;
- therapy models – the concepts, principles and practices that underpin a particular therapeutic approach are extended to the supervision context;
- supervision-specific models – the emphasis is on the roles performed by the supervisor such as the normative, formative and restorative functions described previously;
- pragmatic models – theoretical constructions are de-emphasized in favour of practical considerations such as what works best with a particular client;
- evidence-based models – a specific application of evidence-based practice which aims to combine research with professional consensus on best practice in pursuit of optimum supervisory interventions;
- an eclectic mix of the above.

Of all the supervision approaches employed in therapy practice, developmental models appear to have received the most attention in the literature (McNeill et al. 1992). However, developmental models are not without their critics. Bernard and Goodyear (1992), for example, argued that as an approach to supervision they do not accommodate individual variations in developmental process, account for failures in progression, or consider how practitioners may be more advanced in some domains than others (and thus do not operate at the same level of development across all areas of practice). Milne (2009) also questions their validity, arguing that while they may be intuitively appealing, they are yet to be empirically substantiated. However, there is some merit in developmental models in that they have practical value for personal reflection and can provide a helpful framework for discussing learning needs in supervision.

Stoltenberg (1981) developed a counsellor complexity model which aimed to incorporate a consideration of developmental constructs into the supervision process. In this model, the trainee is believed to progress through a series of stages which ultimately results in the emergence of a personalized counsellor identity.

In a subsequent elaboration, Stoltenberg and Delworth (1987) developed the Integrated Developmental Model (IDM) which attempts to capture therapist progression more effectively. Specifically, they identify three principal structures through which to monitor supervisee development: self and other awareness; motivation; and autonomy. Although the presentation here is necessarily brief, as you read over the three levels identified, see which one most closely resonates with your own career stage:

> Level 1: Supervisees at this level are highly motivated and want to progress rapidly past the anxiety that comes from being a novice. They are relatively dependent on the supervisor, crave concrete answers to the challenges of therapeutic working, and tend to try to imitate expert others, including the supervisor.
>
> Level 2: Supervisees at this level have moved beyond the initial phase of anxiety, resulting in increased focus on the client. This can create confusion, as supervisees have to grapple with therapeutic material in new ways. Simple instructions no longer seem adequate, which can give rise to feelings of ambivalence. This stage is characterized by a dependency–autonomy conflict in which motivation can fluctuate as a function of therapeutic 'successes' and 'failures'.
>
> Level 3: Supervisees at this level are able to achieve both self- and other-awareness. As they begin to develop a personal therapist identity, motivation becomes more stable, there is the capacity for an accurate self-appraisal of strengths and weakness, and a greater capacity for autonomous functioning.

Along complementary lines, a number of authors (e.g. Hess 1980) have proposed that supervisors adopt a series of roles that include lecturer, counsellor, teacher and consultant. Although useful, as Friedlander and Ward (1984) note, they are drawn from contexts other than supervision, which hampers identification of the unique set of skills that underpin optimal supervision. In consequence, Friedlander and Ward examined the dimensions of supervisory style that are perceived as salient both by highly experienced supervisors with diverse orientations and by supervisees at different levels of training. Their study identified three factors: attractive (the collegial dimension of supervision – warm, supportive, friendly, open, flexible); interpersonally sensitive (relationship-orientated approach to supervision – e.g. invested, committed, therapeutic, perceptive); and task-oriented (content-focused – goal-oriented, thorough, focused, practical, structured). Supervisory style was also noted to be multidimensional and associated with theoretical orientation; specifically, task-oriented style was emphasized by cognitive behavioural supervisors and interpersonal style by psychodynamic and humanistic supervisors.

Exercise 24: *Clarifying the Attitude at work in your supervision*

Take a moment to think about the perspectives (the assumptive world, theories or models and styles) that are currently operating in your supervision. How do these shape the issues you discuss in supervision and translate into your subsequent meetings with clients?

Think back to Exercise 22 where you identified a positive and negative experience of supervision. Can you make sense of these experiences drawing on either the broad model of supervision used (developmental, therapy-specific, pragmatic, etc.) or the theoretical stance employed? You might like to organize your dialogue with your supervisor using the following questions:

- Whose perspectives are dominant in supervision? (Supervision can be delivered in different formats – self-supervision, individual, small group, large group, live supervision where the client is present, etc. Which formats are relevant to you and how many people's perspectives will shape what is discussed?)
- What are the perspectives that each party brings to supervision in terms of their values, attitudes and expectations? Their therapy models and approaches? Their foundational assumptions? Distinct therapy models and approaches?
- What are supervisees encouraged and discouraged from talking about, or even attending to, on the basis of the model of supervision used?

Process

Whereas Mission is concerned with supervision contexts, and Attitude is concerned with our perspectives, Process is concerned with what we might term 'supervision interventions', in other words, what an observer might see and hear if they were present. Here, questions about roles and strategies, areas of focus, format and technique, as outlined by Watkins (1997), become paramount.

Currently, relatively little is known about the supervision process and outcomes as influenced by changes in supervisee and supervisor experience or development (see Stoltenberg et al. 1994). Traditionally, researchers in this area have relied heavily on questionnaires that were developed for investigating the counselling process. However, as Stoltenberg et al. (1994) note, supervision differs from counselling in critical ways and some of the key functions of the supervisor (e.g. assessing compe-tence) do not occur in therapy. As such, there remains a lack of broadly applicable measures that inform our understanding of the supervision process.

Nonetheless, there has been considerable growth in the comprehensive-ness of theories and research studies on the supervisory process. Much of this, from early studies onwards, has examined the theoretical approach, supervisory style and format that are most effective for trainees at different stages of their professional development and when working with diverse clinical presentations (Lambert 1980; Hess 1980, respectively).

As part of developmental progression, Stoltenberg and Delworth (1987) have identified how practitioners' capacity for autonomy and self-awareness and their degree of anxiety and confidence need to be accommodated by both the style of supervision and the supervisory meth-ods used. This would appear to be borne out in practice. For example, Stoltenberg et al. (1994) found that supervisors tend to adopt a more task-oriented approach with beginners, and a more interpersonally-oriented approach with more experienced practitioners. This echoes the earlier work of Guest and Beutler (1988) who found that novices particularly appreciate support and instruction on matters of technique. Only as they gain experience do they come to value highly supervisors who hold more complex views of change. For these reasons, Stoltenberg and Delworth (1987) recommend tailoring supervisory strategy to the developmental stage of the supervisee in the following ways:

Level 1: The supervisor needs to encourage autonomy within a nor-mative structure. Instruction in theory, technique and other tasks relevant to professional practice (such as how to conduct an as-sessment or manage risk) should be provided. Structured supervi-sion is needed, along with observation (role-play, playing audio-recordings of therapy sessions in supervision, etc.).

Level 2: What is needed is a balance between structure and support that can accommodate both growing autonomy and the super-visees' awareness of the complexities of practice. Observational methods continue to remain critical to monitoring effectiveness and supervisee development, although there is likely to be less emphasis on direct instruction.

Level 3: The supervisor now needs to avoid an overly structured learn-ing environment, although careful monitoring (through case for-mulations, process notes and reports) remains important. This level can be characterized by a greater openness to feedback and therapeutic process issues.

When calculated in terms of numbers of years of practice, experience is a crude measure of development, and an individual's developmental level is likely to vary across the different domains of therapy (Stoltenberg and Delworth 1987). For example, in group supervision, you may be farther advanced than your peers on matters of assessment, but less experienced in knowing how to deliver particular interventions. Equally, you may find that you prefer a high level of structure and direction when faced with a crisis situation and less structured supervision when exploring a more common therapy dilemma. The supervision strategy you prefer and which your supervisor thinks that you most need (these are not necessarily the same thing) will depend on many factors.

Exercise 25: *Decision-making in the supervision process*

Give some thought to your stage of development as outlined in Stoltenberg and Delworth's (1987) model above. Where would you place yourself at this time? How might this relate to the methods of learning that your supervisor uses? Returning to your most and least helpful experiences of supervision, does this model offer any insights into why you experienced these in the way that you did (e.g. a match or mismatch in your level of experience and the strategy used)?

You might also like to organize your dialogue with your supervisor using the following questions (these relate not only to clarifying your supervisor's expectations of Process but also to the types of methods you might like supervision to include). What are, or will be, the main methods of learning, processes and procedures used in supervision? For example:

- Is there an expectation that you will come with a pre-prepared supervision question about a particular client? Or is the expectation that the most critical issues will be identified as the dialogue unfolds?
- Will you be expected to play audio- or video-recordings of sessions with clients?
- Will experiential exercises such as role-play be used?
- Will your supervisor give demonstrations of specific therapy skills in action?
- In general, what types of strategy support and hinder your learning in supervision?

Pulling it all together

Drawing together some of the key points in this chapter, we offer a list of questions that can support you in using supervision most effectively. For ease of reference, they are organized under the MAP headings.

Mission

1. What is your purpose in supervision? What are you setting out to achieve?
2. What is your supervisor's purpose in supervision? (Do you know? If not, how can you find out?)
3. What is the context in which you and your supervisor are working together? Who or what has had a role in shaping the purpose to your meeting?

Examples of questions relevant to Mission include the following:

(a) Who has negotiated the supervision contract (You? Your training institution? Your local NHS service)? Whose interests are represented in the way the contract has been set up?
(b) What is the service setting in which supervision is taking place? Are there any broader organizational issues (including financial or staffing pressures, excessively high caseloads) that will shape the type of supervision you receive, and the expectations of you as a supervisee? What is the balance of normative, formative and restorative functions in this contract?
(c) Do you know what you want and need from supervision? What qualities, knowledge and skills are you seeking in your supervisor and what underpins this? For example, do you need a supervisor with a specific qualification or registration status for the purposes of your own accreditation, or have you chosen this supervisor because you believe you will work well together?
(d) Who will monitor the quality of the supervision you receive? To whom would you turn if you were unhappy with supervision? Do you have the option of changing supervision if you believed this was necessary?

Attitude

1. What are the perspectives that each party brings to supervision in terms of their values, attitudes, beliefs and expectations?

2. Do you understand the assumptive worlds and therapy models that are likely to be informing your discussions?
3. What will you be encouraged and discouraged from talking about on the basis of the model of supervision used?

Examples of questions relevant to Attitude include the following:

(a) What is your supervisor's framework for understanding human problems?
(b) What theoretical interpretations of your clients' difficulties do they tend to favour?
(c) What does your supervisor feel able and competent to provide? For example, do they specialize in developing a high degree of skill in one particular therapeutic approach, or work within an integrative framework? Can they supervise you on a wide range of client problems or only in one or two specialist areas?
(d) Do you believe that your supervisor understands your stage of development? For example, if you are at the start of your career and in supervision as part of a training placement, are you confident that your supervisor is able to adapt their supervisory style accordingly?

Process

1. How does your supervisor's sense of Mission and Attitude shape their expectations of you in terms of preparing for supervision and what you actually do in your time together?
2. What are the methods, processes and procedures that will be used?
3. What topics, needs and areas of development does the supervisor see as being within and beyond the remit of their role (e.g. personal support during a difficult time, reading course work for feedback prior to submission)? Does this need negotiation?

Examples of questions relevant to Process include the following:

(a) What style of discussion will be used? For example, will there be a strong emphasis on general case management issues, or specific skill acquisition?
(b) What types of learning strategies will be dominant in the sessions – i.e. role-play, instruction on matters of technique, interpretation or use of audio-recordings? Will these supervisory methods remain consistent throughout your work together or will the choice of method evolve as you become more experienced?

(c)   Will you be expected to bring written diagrams of formulations, or drafts of letters to referrers?
(d)   What is agreed in terms of frequency and duration of supervision meetings? Is this enough to meet your needs?

Conclusion

Although there is fairly widespread agreement that supervision is central to therapists' development, there is less agreement as to how it exerts its effects, or which methods are central to optimizing supervisees' development. Milne (2009: 20) refers to the 'awkward gulf' that exists between the aspirations expressed by our professional bodies about the central importance of supervision and the knowledge and material available to develop it. In the main, there is still a lack of formal training opportunities that can enable supervisors to develop and deliver the required competences and no evidence base that can guide supervisors on how to approach their work.

There is an emerging debate about whether supervision should be considered as a distinct professional arena in its own right, that is, a discipline that transcends professional boundaries, rather than an activity involving subject-matter experts instructing their more junior colleagues (the traditional apprenticeship model). These debates are perhaps unlikely to influence what happens when you next meet with your supervisor. Nonetheless, they represent broader contextual factors that will impinge on how supervisors come to understand their identities, roles, and functions in the years to come – and how they will be expected to train and keep their knowledge up to date.

Because of these factors, it is critical to prepare yourself well for any new supervisory relationship. Becoming a therapist is a process of growth that entails developing a sense of authority as an agent of change with something to offer (but not impose upon) your clients. Supervision is central to the task of nurturing this process, but development is not automatically guaranteed. The supervision contract, the context in which it is taking place, the expectations that each party is bringing and the processes used to enhance learning need to be explicit and open to negotiation (or, at the very least, discussion) by all parties involved. In this chapter we have recommended the MAP model as a framework for helping you negotiate the relationship, roles, responsibilities and objectives of supervision more effectively. Ultimately, it is essential that on entering a new supervisory relationship you understand the kind of learning environment that you need and have a role in shaping any agreement about the work that is to follow.

✍ Learning summary

One idea I have found useful in this chapter is. . .

. . . .

. . . .

One thing I would like to experiment with, having read this chapter, is. . .

. . . .

. . . .

Was there anything I didn't quite understand? (If so, I will find out more by. . .)

. . . .

. . . .

9 Decision-making in teams

In this chapter you will learn about:

- the opportunities and challenges afforded by working in a team
- common group processes that can hamper successful decision-making in teams
- processes for enhancing team-based decision-making

By reading this chapter you will be able to:

- evaluate the decision-making capability of the teams in which you work
- capitalize on the learning opportunities provided in teams
- enhance your contribution to team-based discussions

Introduction

Many of the ideas that we have examined in the previous chapters concern decision-making processes and outcomes as they relate to the individual or people in groups. We have considered some of the factors that hold sway over how we decide what to attend to, how we gather data and what we remember. We have also considered how information is subjected to a range of cognitive and emotional manipulations in our consciousness which may be more or less accurate. Although we have considered the way in which a number of external factors may shape how and what we decide (most notably, the influence of cultural, historical, social, economic and professional priorities), we have not yet considered a vital, and increasingly prevalent form of decision-making – namely, that which occurs in teams. This chapter examines some of the factors that are known to influence decision-making in teams and considers ways in which the productivity and success of team decision-making might be enhanced.

> ### Exercise 26: *What is your experience of teams?*
>
> Before reading any further, begin by making a list of the different teams in which you currently work or have worked. Examples may include multidisciplinary community mental health teams, working on an in-patient hospital ward, being a member of a single disciplinary counselling service, or even being part of a non-therapy related team, such as a sales team or board of school governors.
>
> Make a note of any objective or predetermined features about each one, such as its size, the composition of gender, race and culture, regularity of contact and any official mission statement relating to the purpose of the team. Also consider whether its membership is or was relatively stable or characterized by a high turnover. Finally, make a note of whether the team existed in relative isolation from other organizations (e.g. a staff team in a small limited company) or was part of a larger corporate or public sector environment (e.g. a multinational corporation or service sector, such as the National Health Service in Britain).
>
> Make a note of which teams you enjoyed being part of the most, and which ones you enjoyed the least. See if you can identify why each one impacted on you in the way that it did. Also make a note of those teams that you believe functioned most effectively. Then make a note of those teams that you believe functioned least effectively. Do you have any hypotheses about which factors might have been operating in each case?
>
> As you read through the chapter, make a note of any ideas that might help you better understand the teams in which you have worked in the past or are working in now.

Why is team decision-making so important to understand?

In recent decades, team working has become increasingly prevalent in employment settings. Many organizations now rely on teams to create new knowledge, develop innovative products and services, solve complex problems and find ways to achieve better results with fewer resources (Kayes 2006). Indeed, Guzzo and Shea (1992) report that in organizations comprising more than 100 employees, over 80 per cent rely on teams. There is, as Hardman (2009) points out, a prevailing belief that the diversity in teams will lead to more creative and better decisions. However, the evidence he examines indicates that while they can be effective decision units, teams often fail. In consequence, we need to understand how teams function, how individuals function within teams, and what enables and disables decision-making in these settings.

As a vehicle for both decision-making and service delivery, the ability of individuals to function effectively as team members has become a prerequisite skill of many professions (Stevens and Campion 1994). Perhaps for this reason, team learning has become more prevalent in education, reflected in the increased use of student learning teams (Light 2001), assignments where a student's final grade is dependent upon team performance (Chen et al. 2004) and team supervision (Hawkins 2011). Learning team work skills is undoubtedly an essential competence for securing and sustaining employment and developing your career.

Team work can take many forms and can vary across a range of dimensions. Teams can be single- or cross-functional, time-limited or enduring, and manager-led or self-led, according to the culture and priorities of the organization as a whole.

Perhaps the most frequently encountered teams – at least for therapists – are those that operate at 'grass-roots level' making decisions about the services required by individual clients and how best to deliver these services. A typical example would be the multidisciplinary community mental health team where clients referred to the service might be assessed by one individual but where the offer of care will reflect the decision-making of the team as a whole during a referrals meeting.

There are also teams whose membership comprises those united for a more specific and time-limited purpose – such as to identify services for the purposes of income generation or who are seconded to a task-specific project team in order to pursue a specialist area. Examples might be individuals who come together to function as an expert panel, such as when training courses apply for formal recognition or accreditation with a professional body, or when recognized experts combine their knowledge and skills to support the development of treatment guidelines for a particular disorder.

Team work also refers to those who make strategic decisions at senior management and board level. Here, membership will be restricted to those whose experience and rank qualify them (it is assumed) to understand the broader issues at stake, and whose decisions will cascade through the organization and influence the working lives of their subordinates.

Regardless of the differences in their structure, purpose and function, all organizational work teams share the following properties: they exist within a larger organization; they have clearly defined membership; and they share responsibility for a service or product (Hackman 2002).

A review of the teams in which you have operated is likely to reveal the impact of a range of teams – those in which you are involved day-to-day and those which exert a more distal (but potentially equally impactful) influence on your practice. One example of this might be the impact on a local authority housing project (a team attempting to address the needs of its local community) of public sector cuts in spending decided by central government.

Working in teams may offer a number of advantages, including the potential to 'iron out' some of the decision-making biases we examined in Chapter 1. The explicit sharing of ideas and the thinking behind them has the potential to enable the team to identify and correct any distortions or inaccuracies that may be occurring through discussion, respectful challenge and the offering of different perspectives. There is also the potential for team discussion to generate options that the individual alone would be unlikely to produce. Based on the notion of a Gestalt whereby the whole is greater than the sum of its parts, the potential of high-functioning teams is to create an environment whereby discussions can be more informative; the ideas generated more varied, sophisticated and exhaustive; heuristics and other cognitive biases minimized (through the corrective function of group discourse and constructive challenge); and the implication and evaluation of a subsequent decision more closely evaluated. Where teams function in this way, undoubtedly the success of the decision-making that affects our clients is likely to increase.

Team functioning is not without its challenges. It has been well documented that many individuals who work in teams find the experience unsatisfactory, consider team discussion an unnecessary and unproductive use of time, or feel constrained by the limitations of other members' thinking and skill. In life-critical situations this can lead to poor and fatal decision-making – see Krakauer (1998) on mountaineering, and Bureau of Air Safety Investigation (1996) on aviation. In the context of education, sources of dissatisfaction tend to include complaints from students that not all members are willing to carry out their share of the work, although benefiting from the work of others, creating the potential for resentment and conflict.

These opportunities and challenges raise important questions about what makes teams function more or less effectively, and in particular the factors that influence their decision-making capability. In the next section, we consider some of the findings in the literature that can assist us in understanding these processes more fully.

What makes teams more or less effective? Insights on group processes from social psychology

As Paul and Elder (2002) point out, human beings are sociocentric by nature and as such are easily drawn into sociocentric thinking and behaviour. Through internalizing and uncritically conforming to their culture and rules, social groups offer us a measure of security and belonging, and hence set the parameters which define our worlds.

In the social psychology of groups and group functioning, a number of detrimental forms of influence have been identified that are clearly relevant to both team performance and team member satisfaction (see Hardman 2009). Specifically, teams can fall prey to decision-making short-cuts and biases in the same way in which individuals are affected. Some of the more prevalent dysfunctional psychological processes, along with a brief description and illustrative example of each, are listed in Table 3. See if

Table 3 Common psychological processes that occur in groups

Social loafing	Where people make less effort in pursuit of a goal, when they are working in a group as opposed to working alone. Example: you are in a referrals meeting in a service where there is considerable pressure to reduce waiting-list times. You notice that one or two people always remain quiet when the referrals manager asks who has the space to assess a new client.
Groupthink	Where groups make decisions too quickly, based on the desire to reach a consensus of viewpoint rather than engage in critical thinking. As a result, the group is prone to faulty decisions through a deterioration of 'mental efficiency, reality testing, and moral judgment' (Janis 1972: 9). Example: you are in a group where there have been some difficult issues about handling referrals but a sense that the team needs to change. Someone makes a suggestion which has not been fully thought through but is seized upon by two members as it appears to be a solution. Other members gradually take up the same position and the idea is adopted without critical examination – largely because it releases the tension that was present.
Abilene paradox	Summarized by the desire to avoid 'rocking the boat', and possibly a variation of the groupthink phenomenon, the Abilene paradox occurs when a group collectively decides on a course of action that is inconsistent with the preferences of the individuals in the group. Individual members believe (inaccurately) that their own preferences differ from group opinion and as a result fail to raise any objections or challenge the decision made (Harvey 1996). This finding suggests that human beings are typically reluctant to make decisions or act in ways that are contrary to the trend of the group. Example: team members are discussing an 'away-day team-building' session. Someone suggests paintballing (it is mid-winter). In their thoughts most people are hesitant but agree that it is a good idea, believing that others will think it is great fun – so paintballing is chosen, which most really do not want to do.

(Continued)

Table 3 (*Continued*)

Group polarization	The way in which, following any decision or judgement, groups tend to shift in the direction of the position which they favour initially; an intensification of an initially dominant position or viewpoint due to group discussion (e.g. Myers 2005). This can occur through conformity to powerful positions, rehearsal of familiar positions, or shift to a majority position to gain group approval (Isenberg 1986). Example: in a team meeting you are considering new ways to track your work. An initial suggestion seems to be favoured by key members, but efforts to explore alternatives are largely superficial and the initial tracking suggestion is adopted.
Risky shift	A variation of group polarization whereby people in groups tend to make decisions about risk differently from when deciding alone. Specifically, this refers to the notion that groups generally make riskier decisions than individuals (Stoner 1961). Note, however, that some studies have shown the opposite effect (e.g. Moscovici and Zavalloni 1969). This is a more extreme version of group polarization. Example: faced with a choice between two options, one with lesser but more secure reward and one with higher risk but possible greater reward, individuals choosing alone opted for the former but in group discussion selected the latter, riskier option – the group shifted the risk choice.

you can identify whether any of these may have been operating in the teams in which you have worked, particularly those where you have observed difficulties in team functioning or have experienced dissatisfaction as a team member.

Exercise 27: *Therapist dilemma. What would you do?*

You are a newly qualified practitioner working as part of a multidisciplinary community mental health team. As is typical, the team comprises some very experienced practitioners in the fields of psychiatry, psychology, mental health nursing, occupational therapy and social work. Generally, you enjoy working as part of the team and respect your colleagues' experience and expertise. You are its most junior member.

Following a case presentation, a decision is made to close a client's file and refer him back to the GP. The discussion particularly revolves around whether or not the client meets the service's criteria for severe and enduring mental illness. Ultimately, the conclusion is that he does not and so his needs are best met through passing the referral back to the client's GP for support through another service. You do not agree with this decision and believe that the client could be at risk of self-harm and would benefit from the containment that team input could offer. You suspect that the team is being unduly influenced by outside pressure to cut costs and by a desire to protect service boundaries in the context of a major organizational restructuring. However, you are the least experienced member of the team and, being fairly new, you need to secure your place within it.

Think for a moment about how this situation would impact on you and what reactions you might have on both an intellectual and an emotional level. Think about your stage of career development, your reputation among your colleagues, your knowledge of your own cognitive biases and decision-making style, and your tacit beliefs or schema about therapy and therapeutic services to clients. Then, taking account of all of these factors, consider the following questions:

- What would you do?
- What would you not do?
- What factors would be most influential in shaping your decision? Why?
- What factors would be least influential in shaping your decision? Why?

If you have been honest, you will probably have recognized at the very least the temptation of falling victim to one of the phenomena highlighted previously. Make a note in your learning log, and particularly note any of the influencers that you might need to watch out for in the future.

As teams have become a dominant means through which organizations deliver their services, so the literature has begun to draw a distinction between groups and teams, and to begin to examine those structures, processes and tasks that are indicative of team functioning within organizations, rather than other types of groups.

Although an appreciation of group processes is an essential starting point to understanding the factors that might inhibit decision-making in teams, groups and teams are not necessarily the same thing and it is important to distinguish between working as part of a team and working as part of a group.

Members of the latter are effectively independent in terms of their workload. In teams, however, there is a high level of interdependency; one member cannot complete their work without the others' input. Kayes (2006) explains this distinction by using the example of people who fly as airline passengers. He suggests that these individuals can be understood as forming a group because they share the common goal of arriving at a particular location. However, although the passengers are united by a desired outcome, they are not interdependent – they do not share the means to bring about or hinder the outcome which is typical of team functioning. For example, as an airline passenger, it is commonplace to experience an entire flight having had no communication with most or all of the other passengers; the passengers merely exist as a group of individuals who happen to come together with the same outcome in mind. In contrast, the cockpit and cabin crews function as a team; they share both the common goal (arriving safely at the correct destination) and the means (including, in the case of the pilots, the expertise of flying) to achieve it. Moreover, they have to function as an interdependent unit in order to fulfil their purpose.

This analogy may have some limitations, but we find it useful for considering the interdependencies that form in team working and how these might impact on practitioners' decision-making capability. In the next section we develop this by drawing on the work of theorists and researchers who have identified the impact of an additional set of factors that are at work in teams.

Understanding how teams function

Although much has been written about teams, relatively little is known about how they actually work, the mechanisms by which they learn and the means through which they attain optimal effectiveness (Edmondson 1999; Kayes 2006). Edmondson (2002) has argued that the relationship between cognitive and social learning processes and how these manifest as team learning remains unclear. Equally, she highlights the lack of information about whether team learning occurs in the moment or develops over time and the processes by which an environment of psychological safety is created.

Some studies have demonstrated that team effectiveness is enhanced through structural features, such as having clear and well-designed tasks, appropriate team composition and a context that ensures the necessary information, resources and rewards are in place (Hackman 2002; for a review, see Kozlowski and Ilgen 2006). Indeed, a number of researchers have argued that structure and design – including the availability of appropriate materials, the physical environment and pay systems – are the key factors implicated in improving team performance and that it is not appropriate to consider focusing on interpersonal factors (e.g. Cohen and Ledford 1994). Other studies have emphasized the importance of cognitive and interpersonal factors in explaining team effectiveness. In particular, organizational learning research (e.g. Argyris 1993) proposes that individuals' tacit beliefs about interpersonal interaction can prevent adaptive learning behaviour and thus contribute to organizational ineffectiveness.

Given the highly dynamic nature of teams, quite apart from the increasingly complex settings in which they provide clinical services, it is perhaps unsurprising that the literature offers only a limited understanding of team functioning. Drawing on examples of team working occurring in seemingly unrelated fields might, therefore, prove helpful in clarifying some of the complexities in teams operating in the therapeutic and mental health professions. Here, Kayes (2006) presents us with a particularly compelling illustration of a range of detrimental factors at work.

Drawing on the 1996 Mount Everest climbing disaster as a framework for developing his thesis, Kayes (2006) examines the series of critical errors in decision-making that the leaders of the expedition made, with catastrophic consequences. In the context of goal-setting, he attempts to address the reasons why the leaders persisted with pursuing their goal of reaching the summit, given the mounting evidence that it could not be achieved.

In extrapolating the lessons of the Everest disaster for decision-making in organizations, Kayes proposes that we need to understand the realities of decision-making as comprising a series of human dilemmas that involve what he terms 'uneasy choices that often result in unsatisfactory outcomes' (2006: xxi). When goals become the exclusive driver for action, destructive goal pursuit – a phenomenon he terms 'goalodicy' – occurs. At such times, goals provide the justification of action (to self and others) and 'become difficult to abandon, provide a handy language to justify undesirable action, lead to unintended consequences, and under some conditions lead to unethical behaviour' (2006: 36).

The over-commitment to goals that Kayes argues is so problematic, would perhaps be regarded by some as almost heretical. After all, even a cursory glance at almost any personal development book will support the supremacy of goal setting in almost all areas of performance enhancement, including a number of therapeutic approaches. Clear, operationalized and measurable goals have been proposed as essential to clarity of purpose and of focus, and a method that enhances the likelihood of success (Locke and Latham 1990), and represent what could be seen to be a 'foundational assumption' (see Chapter 2) of the western approach to personal development.

Indeed, when problems are circumscribed and achievable through effort alone then goal-setting is highly effective. However, this approach relies on having a well-structured and clearly defined problem and a means to achieve the goal. Many of the challenges we face in teams constitute, in Kayes' terms, ill-structured problems, rendering the goal unclear. This in turn inevitably leads to a lack of clarity around the means necessary to achieve the goal and also what would constitute success. Of the dilemmas that he identifies as critical to organizations at this time, many would be descriptive of the teams in which therapists work, including:

- pressure to achieve ever higher standards with limited resources;
- increased use of rigid outcome performance criteria;
- greater competition (rather than co-operation) between agencies;
- drive towards short-term performance (including, we might add, fire fighting) rather than long-term strategic planning);
- multicultural environments;
- delivering services in an unpredictable climate.

Exercise 28: *Putting it to the test: does Kayes's theory fit your experience?*

Think back to a time when you were part of a team. Remember a time when this team was successful in achieving a goal. Recall what the goal was – make sure that it was a goal that really mattered to the team and which required some degree of effort and persistence. Remember the details as vividly as you can. Was it a well- or ill-defined problem? How did the team approach the goal? How specific were you all about what you wanted to achieve? The means of achieving it? How able were you to accurately evaluate your progress? How attached were you to the goal? In what circumstances would you have chosen to abandon it?

Now think of a time when, despite all good intentions, the team was unsuccessful in achieving a goal. Again, make sure that this was a goal that really mattered to you and which required some degree of effort and persistence. Remember the details as vividly as you can. Was it a well- or ill-defined problem? How did the team approach the goal? How specific were you all about what you wanted to achieve? The means of achieving it? How able were you to accurately evaluate your progress? How attached were you to the goal? In what circumstances would you have chosen to abandon it?

Does Kayes's notion of 'goalodicy' fit any of the experiences you have had, individually or as part of a team, in relation to goal setting and decision-making?

Improving your team's thinking: solutions to these challenges

Where individuals and teams are confronted with complex, multi-faceted problems in rapidly evolving circumstances for which there is no single correct solution, the challenges facing teams may require a unique approach. Faced with such competing pressures, Kayes proposes that it is *team learning*, rather than goal setting, that needs to be developed.

Chapman (2010), drawing on the work of Bunker and Alban (1997), argues that teams need to create:

- room for decision-making;
- opportunity to learn (and keep learning) on the job;
- variety;
- mutual support and respect;
- meaningfulness;
- a desirable future.

In a recent study of high-performing teams, Hawkins (2011) outlined the five disciplines that teams need to get right in order to function effectively:

1. A clear commission for the work to be undertaken.
   - Does your team have a clear commission? Do you know what is expected by those who commissioned the team?
2. Clarification internally by the team of its primary purpose, goals, objectives and roles.
   - How are you going to create *together* clarity for the whole team and thereby ownership of your purpose and responsibilities?
3. Co-creation of the working process.
   - Having a clear commission and purpose is a starting point, but the team needs to *constantly* attend to how they work together, so how will you monitor your functioning?
4. Connecting individually and collectively.
   - How will you make a difference through engaging with all your critical stakeholders?
5. Core learning to support all the other disciplines.
   - How will you stand back and reflect on your performance and incorporate multiple processes to consolidate your learning to gain the best from this engagement and prepare for the next cycle?

Hawkins (2011) makes the point that all five disciplines have to be present, that they are cyclical, not linear, and that they require internal flow between all disciplines.

Questions to guide analysis of your team's decision-making capability

Teams have their own culture, rules and decision-making processes. Spend some time reflecting on the culture of the team or teams of which you are currently a member. Then consider the following questions:

1. Is your team high or low in psychological safety and trust? (Clues: How are mistakes responded to? How often is there constructive disagreement in the sharing of ideas? Are discussions open? Are there small subgroups within the team that tend to engage in malicious gossip about others?)
2. How do your team members listen to one another? To what extent are there opportunities for open and reflective listening?
3. How often do you find yourself inwardly disagreeing with the decisions made by your team, but going along with them anyway, or at the very least remaining silent?
4. What are the learning styles of the different team members? Is there convergence or divergence?
5. At what stage of development is the team?

Conclusion

Teams are now a key part of most people's working lives. As a result, we need to develop ways of better understanding how teams function, the processes through which they arrive at their decisions, and some of the challenges that can impede successful decision-making in these contexts.

There is a growing body of research on group processes that has identified a range of group phenomena that can prevent successful decision-making and, at extreme levels, lead to what Kayes (2006) has described as 'destructive goal pursuit'. There are, however, ways to improve team thinking and evidence that adopting appropriate frameworks does result in higher-performing teams.

Adopting the type of decision tools we have described in this chapter is based on the assumption that there is a shared Mission in operation. However, it is important to remember that this is not always the case and not all work groups function as teams. It is important to be aware of the type of collective in which you are working and whether, based on the ideas presented in this chapter, this is best understood as a team or work group.

Finally, before we conclude this chapter, take some time to complete Exercise 29 and make a note of any relevant points in your learning log.

Exercise 29: *Planning your future performance as a team member*

Review your responses to Exercise 26 at the start of this chapter. If you think back over your experience of working in teams, which factors would you rate as being most important in what helped or hindered team functioning? Which factors were most implicated in your evaluation of each team being effective or ineffective? What ideas discussed in this chapter might you want to hold in mind for your future performance as a team member? How might you now plan with your team to enhance decision-making capability?

✍ Learning summary

One idea I have found useful in this chapter is. . .

. . . .

. . . .

One thing I would like to experiment with, having read this chapter, is. . .

. . . .

. . . .

Was there anything I didn't quite understand? (If so, I will find out more by. . .)

. . . .

. . . .

10 Developing as a critical thinker: some final recommendations

Helping individuals become effective thinkers has been recognized as a major goal of education for some time (see, for example, Cotton 1991). Although a number of authors have identified decision-making as a goal of therapist training (see Bernard and Goodyear 2004; Owen and Lindley 2010), this continues to be a neglected topic in the psychotherapy and counselling literatures. There remains a paucity of guidance on how therapists should develop these skills and how those involved in supervision and training can facilitate them.

From having read this book, it will be clear to the reader that we see the capacity to develop successful decision-making skills as a discipline in its own right. Critical thinking skills are essential for individuals to be able to manage the demands of a rapidly changing world where the decisions required may involve swift and sometimes cross-disciplinary responses. To become proficient in the mental operations required of practitioners involves more than just discipline-specific knowledge, or a sound awareness of the latest evidence. It also requires the orchestration of distinct mindsets that include curiosity, openness and a genuine commitment to enhancing personal learning and self-knowledge.

Becoming a better thinker also requires courage. It is not easy to expose our habitual thinking to a process of scrutiny – doing so inevitably brings us face to face with our own intellectual limitations, prejudices, flawed beliefs, irrational cognitive processes and taken-for-granted assumptions of which we may have been only partially aware. As a result, if you truly engaged with the exercises in this book you may have found some of the exercises difficult, uncomfortable or even unsettling as you grappled to understand why you hold certain views and the implications of these for you, your clients and your role as a professional. You might even have found yourself having to question aspects of your style of working with which you had formerly felt quite comfortable. If this is true for you, then we would suggest that you are most definitely on the right lines! Until such time as you are prepared to reflect deeply on your approach to decision-making, you will continue to be swayed by the prejudices of the day and remain unaware of the impact of the foundational assumptions of your chosen profession and the cultures in which you live and work.

The painter and media artist Marcel Duchamp is quoted as saying, 'I force myself into self-contradiction to avoid following my taste' (Buckland 1999). We would offer this as useful advice for acquiring and refining successful decision-making skills. By committing yourself to the regular practice of challenging your own views, you prevent yourself from becoming so enmeshed in your own schemas that they become beyond question.

The assumptions that have underpinned this book

Recognizing that we, as authors of this book, are also students of the discipline of critical thinking, it is only right and proper that we open up our own approach to scrutiny. In the service of this, what follows is a summary of some of the key assumptions that have underpinned the ideas we have presented, the literatures we have drawn upon and the exercises we have offered you as a means of developing your decision-making skills. This section can also serve to refresh your memory of some of the core ideas and approaches covered.

Some of the key assumptions that have informed our thinking are as follows:

1. Following Gambrill (2005), we believe that critical thinking is an intellectually and, at times, emotionally demanding enterprise. This is because in order to pave the way for new ideas, we must excavate, analyse and ultimately eliminate old ones – ones to which we may actually be quite attached.
2. In the real world decisions are often complex. The dilemmas faced by practitioners new to the profession are also shared with more experienced colleagues because decision-making is not easy.
3. It is possible to learn to become a better decision-maker through taking a 'meta-perspective' (holistic view) in which we move from specific tools acquired in life or training to further tools drawn from the literature on decision-making. There are ways to improve the accuracy of our decision-making. However, the best decision is not always the most accurate decision. Accuracy always has to be balanced with helpfulness, as there are broader issues (such as ethical dilemmas, client engagement or risk management issues) of which we need to take account.
4. In order to make successful decisions, we need to be able to operate from a range of styles of reasoning. Those that are concerned

with technical knowledge call for accuracy of judgement, and those that are concerned with innovation call for creativity, intuition, felt sense and an ability to design novel solutions to new challenges.

5. Decisions are context-bound; they are not just about individual decision-making skills but also about what is possible in the context in which we work.
6. In the real world events may be simple, complicated, complex or chaotic – we need to adjust our decision-making approach according to the requirements of these different 'spaces'.
7. Understanding the nature of events in these different spaces enables a better match between the events and the decision tools we have available to understand them.
8. There are some useful tools that can address complexity (some of these are simple, and some are more difficult to learn, but are worth the effort!)
9. Working with these powerful tools requires a real engagement with self-awareness and an ongoing commitment to becoming an effective thinker. Successful decision-making is a lifelong endeavour, not a skill that can be acquired once and for all.

With these foundational assumptions clearly stated, let us now recap on the rationale for MAP.

Expanding your horizons: why you need a MAP

To be a therapist is to live and work in a place of ambiguity. The advancements in theoretical and technical knowledge that have characterized the field of therapy in recent decades have provided us with important – even inspiring – information and can unquestionably assist us in making better decisions with, and for, our clients. Nevertheless there is no escaping the fact that therapeutic work consistently immerses us in often high levels of uncertainty and confronts us with difficult questions to which there can be no easy answer.

Human beings are complex and our thoughts, feelings and actions do not always lend themselves well to simplistic explanations. Nor do the service settings in which we find ourselves. It is for this reason that we have resisted the temptation of providing simplistic formulae for therapeutic decisions in real-world contexts. Decision-making techniques exist in abundance and can be very useful in situations where all the relevant factors are known and the outcomes are predictable. However, they are less relevant to the more complex and multifaceted decisions with which therapy often confronts us. In consequence, we need to be wary of attempts (however well intentioned) that appear to supply simplistic formulae to complex issues; the reassurance they provide may ultimately prove illusory.

As Bandura and Schunk (1981: 587) point out:

> Competence in dealing with one's environment is not a fixed act or simply knowing what to do. Rather, it involves a generative capability in which component skills must be selected and organized into integrated courses of action to manage changing task demands. Operative competence thus requires flexible orchestration of multiple subskills.

Paul (1993), along similar lines, suggests that in order to become effective critical thinkers, the task is one of unhooking from the *content* of our decisions in order to examine, more impartially, the *process* by which we arrive at them – it is the integrity of the Process which is essential and which, over time, can enable us to have confidence that we have acquired a sound approach to making decisions, regardless of the context in which we are working.

We find these arguments to be compelling. If we focus, in Bandura and Schunk's (1981) terms, on developing a framework for enhancing 'generative capability' rather than looking for ways to undertake a 'fixed act', and take seriously Paul's claim that we need to focus on the process rather than content of any decision-making activity, then the rationale for having a clear decision-making framework becomes apparent. In the service of focusing on the integrity of our decision-making process we have, in this book, introduced you to MAP which can assist you in being clear about the fundamental purpose of the work that is to be undertaken (your Mission), the perspectives or 'fields of vision' that shape how the therapy unfolds (your Attitude), and the methods, tools, procedures and techniques needed to achieve the contract agreed with the client (your Process).

In an attempt to capture the challenges of decision-making in different types of service context, we have also used the analogy of different 'spaces' or quadrants. Although, in reality, a particular practice setting may contain elements of more than one of these quadrants, the analogy can be useful in sifting through the wealth of information, ideas, assumptions, values and prejudices that may confront you when working in any given setting. By making sense of them, you can begin to consider your options and the different approaches to decision-making that may help you navigate your context more effectively. The different quadrants we have considered (in relation to how these shape Mission, Attitudes and Process) are as follows:

Quadrant 1 (individual and known)	We are seekers after an individual truth to decide what will work for this client in this context.
Quadrant 2 (collective and known)	We can draw upon a collective understanding of the client's issues; we have an evidence base to enable us to structure our decisions.
Quadrant 3 (collective and unknown)	We are faced with a collective need or competing needs in a social system with no agreed understanding or knowledge base on which to draw; we cannot agree what to do for the best.
Quadrant 4 (individual and unknown)	We are faced with an individual journey into the unknown; neither client nor therapist knows what might be appropriate, how to generate change or if change is needed.

Recognizing which of the quadrants is most relevant to your current work setting also enables you to consider some important questions about your readiness to work in such a context. As we discussed previously, some of these quadrants are easier to navigate than others. So we would recommend that you get into the habit of asking yourself the following questions:

- Am I clear about what I want to achieve?
- Am I clear about the relevant factors for undertaking this particular piece of work at this particular point in time?
- Do I have the available resources – internal and external; technical and intuitive?
- If not, what are my options?

Identifying your next steps as a critical thinker: a reflective tool for refining your decision-making potential

Throughout this book we have offered a range of exercises, each of which can support you in reflecting upon, critiquing and developing a specific mindset, style of reasoning or thinking skill. These exercises have often taken the form of questions. This is for a good reason. As Williams (1999) observes, the aim of any meaningful enquiry is less about arriving at clear-cut answers than about being willing to entertain the question in a way that enables us to become clear about its true meaning and implications for our lives. Questions can help signpost key debates and personalize the ideas to our own individual circumstances and needs. They can support the development of our decision-making capability by encouraging us to consider the work we do from new angles and thus assist us with career planning.

For this reason, we conclude this book with what we term 'a reflective tool'. This tool takes the form of a series of questions that relate to the different components of MAP as well as some of the debates drawn from the wider literature that we have discussed. We would recommend that you use these ideas creatively and repeatedly and that you share your ideas with colleagues, peers, supervisors and trainers to turn them into a lived reality that has implications for your future as a highly successful decision-maker.

Your reflective tool

1. *Having read all the different chapters and reflected on their content, what do you now know about your decision-making abilities?*
   (a) What is best/most successful about your decision-making approach?
   (b) What is worst/least successful about your decision-making approach?
   (c) Which specific areas would it make most sense to work on for the immediate future (e.g. accuracy? innovation? elucidating your Mission or Attitude?)
2. *In which decision-making areas are you most likely to feel challenged? If you were to undertake an audit of your practice so far, would you tend to feel most challenged when having to make decisions about:*
   (a) The nature of the problem or concern that needs to be the focus of therapy?

(b) How to make sense of this (what we might refer to as devising a formulation of a client's needs in which you link theory, evidence and the client's story to make sense of the case)?

(c) The optimum approach to goal setting?

(d) What type of intervention might be best suited to the client's needs?

(e) How to implement an intervention plan?

(f) How to evaluate progress (evident, for example, if there is a tendency for your clients to end therapy unexpectedly)?

(g) How to manage unexpected events in therapy (such as a client making a self-disclosure that poses an ethical dilemma for you)?

(h) Some other area (specify)?

Spend some time thinking about your responses to these questions and see if you can come up with examples of where and how these dilemmas have presented themselves in your practice with a range of clients. How might you use MAP to support you in navigating this area of personal challenge more effectively?

3. *How confident are you in the accuracy of your decisions?*

Given all of the decision-making biases we have discussed in this book, it is perhaps best to remain cautious about the accuracy of our judgements – at least as a general rule. A simple task that we would recommend to help you with this is to get into the habit of examining your sessions with clients for the source of the information on which you are basing your judgements. (If you can audio-record your sessions this task is much easier.) Spend some time reflecting on your actions and reactions and attempt to clarify what you thought, felt and did based on the following classification:

(a) What did I observe (i.e. actually see)?

(b) What did I hear (i.e. what was actually said, any periods of silence, etc.)?

(c) What did I infer (i.e. assumptions, interpretations, judgements)?

Make a note of how much information you have under each heading. Are they equally balanced or not? Are any of the categories missing key pieces of information? If you have more information under the 'inference' heading than the others, this may be a sign that you are relying more on your personal epistemology than the actual data of your senses. This may or may not be problematic, but it is worth taking to supervision to discuss further.

4. *Which styles of reasoning do you use the most and least?*
    In this book we have differentiated propositional and implicational forms of knowing. The former refers to information that is relatively abstract and can usually be evaluated for its accuracy. The latter refers to a more holistic form of knowing in which information is deeply meaningful and personal to us. In therapy:
    (a) How comfortable are you with propositional styles of reasoning?
    (b) How comfortable are you with implicational styles of reasoning?
    (c) How comfortable are you with using technical information to guide your decision-making?
    (d) How comfortable are you with using 'felt sense' information to guide your decision-making?

5. *What is the MAP that has governed your approach so far?*
    Spend some time reflecting on the journey that has led you to become a therapist (or to want to become one). What are the factors from your personal and professional story that have shaped your understanding of therapy and the factors that you believe are important to consider? Here are some questions to guide you:
    (a) What influences have shaped your learning journey as a therapist?
    (b) As you look back over your life and career so far, what do you consider to be your most significant achievements? What resources did you bring to bear to achieve these ends (in terms of reasoning style, thinking skills and decision-making approaches) and what did you learn from them?
    (c) What have been the major challenges in your work? How have you attempted to manage these (in terms of reasoning style, thinking skills and decision-making approaches) and what have you learned from them?
    (d) In terms of how to make decisions, what learning have you gained from formal education?
    (e) In terms of how to make decisions, what learning have you gained from experience?
    (f) What is your personal epistemology (i.e. the tapestry of beliefs you hold about what knowledge is and how to obtain it, what type of knowledge you think is appropriate for your professional practice and how you have used it in the past)? How does this influence (and how much is it influenced by) the

perspectives that are dominant in your preferred therapeutic approach?

(g) What is your personal ontology (i.e. how your experience and learning to date have impacted on how you view the world and act within it)?

(h) Based on your experience so far, what is your preferred therapeutic approach? What assumptions about human nature, distress and change come with this perspective? What are the strengths and limitations of these foundational assumptions? To what types of decisions does this approach give rise?

(i) What future direction do you wish your professional development to take?

Spend some time mulling over your responses and see if you can probe these experiences in order to access their deeper meaning and implications for how you live and work. What can you learn from your responses about how you approach therapy? Is there anything that you would like to change for this next stage of your career? Write down your responses in your learning log.

A final thought

The purpose of this book is to help you become more successful at decision-making, as a route to making better choices more often. This will benefit not only your clients and the services which employ you, but also yourself. We genuinely believe that by becoming better thinkers we can improve not only the quality of the services we provide but also the satisfaction we experience through offering them.

We live and work in unprecedented times. Professionals offer their services to clients in organizational, social and economic contexts that are characterized by increasing levels of complexity, uncertainty and turbulence. The challenges that confront us and the decisions we need to make in such a climate are also likely to become increasingly complex. We cannot assume that the technical knowledge and evidence of today will prove fit for purpose for the needs of tomorrow. However, we can ready ourselves for the challenges ahead by committing ourselves to the lifelong discipline of critical thinking.

By writing this book, we hope to assist you in critiquing your own decision-making capability and to support you in deciding where your lifelong learning might need to be headed next. Wherever you are in your career, wherever you work and whatever type of therapy you provide, we hope that this book will be a reliable companion for the many decisions that lie ahead and arouse your interest and curiosity in your own mental operations. We wish you well on your journey.

References

Adair, J. (2010) *Decision Making and Problem Solving Strategies*. London: Kogan Page.

Anderson, H. and Swim, S. (1995) Supervision as collaborative conversation: the voices of supervisor and supervisee, *Journal of Systemic Therapies*, 14(2): 1–13.

Argyris, C. (1993) *Knowledge in Action*. San Francisco, CA: Jossey-Bass.

Arkes, H.R. (1981) Impediments to accurate clinical judgment and possible ways to minimize their impact, *Journal of Consulting and Clinical Psychology*, 49(3): 323–30.

Bandura, A. and Schunk, D.H. (1981) Cultivating competence, self-efficacy, and intrinsic interest through proximal self-motivation, *Journal of Personality and Social Psychology*, 41: 586–98.

Baxter Magolda, M.B. (2009) Promoting self-authorship to promote liberal education, *Journal of College & Character*, X(3): 1–6.

Becher, E.C. and Chassin, M.R. (2001) Improving quality, minimizing error: making it happen, *Health Affairs*, 20(3): 68–81.

Beck, A.T., Rush, A.J., Shaw, B.F. and Emery, G. (1979) *Cognitive Therapy of Depression*. New York: Guilford.

Benedetti, J. (1999) *Stanislavski: His Life and Art*. London: Methuen.

Bernard, J.M. and Goodyear, R.K. (1992) *Fundamentals of Clinical Supervision*. Boston, MA: Allyn and Bacon.

Bernard, J.M. and Goodyear, R.K. (2004) *Fundamentals of Clinical Supervision*, 3rd edn. Boston, MA: Allyn and Bacon.

Beyer, B.K. (1985) Critical thinking: what is it? *Social Education*, 49: 270–6.

Bieling, P.J. and Kuyken, W. (2003) Is cognitive formulation science or science fiction? *Clinical Psychology: Science and Practice*, 10(1): 52–69.

Blackburn, I.M., James, I.A., Milne, D.L., Baker, C., Standart, S., Garland, A. and Reichelt, K. (2001) The revised cognitive therapy scale (CTS-R): psychometric properties, *Behavioural and Cognitive Psychotherapy*, 29: 431–46.

Bonosky, N. (1995) Boundary violations in social work supervision: clinical educational and legal implications, *Clinical Supervisor*, 13: 79–95.

Bowlby, J. (1988) *A Secure Base: Clinical Applications of Attachment Theory*. London: Routledge.

Brewin, C.R. (1989) Attribution, emotion and counselling psychology. In D.A. Lane (ed.), *Attributions, Beliefs and Constructs in Counselling Psychology*. Leicester: British Psychological Society, pp. 7–12.

British Association for Counselling and Psychotherapy (2010) *Ethical Framework for Good Practice in Counseling and Psychotherapy*. Lutterworth: BACP. http://www.bacp.co.uk/admin/structure/files/pdf/566_ethical_framework_feb2010.pdf

British Psychological Society (2006) *Continuous Supervision*. Leicester: BPS.

British Psychological Society (2011) *Register of Applied Psychology Practice Supervisors*. http://www.bps.org.uk/what-we-do/developing-profession/register-applied-psychology-practice-supervisors-rapps/register-app (accessed 14 September 2011).

Bruner, J.S. (1987) Life as narrative. *Social Research*, 54(1): 11–32.

Bruner, J.S. (1990) *Acts of Meaning*. Cambridge, MA: Harvard University Press.

Buber, M. (1937) *I and Thou*. London: Continuum.

Buckland, D. (1999) *David Buckland Performances*. London: D.B. Publications.

Bunker, B.B. and Alban, B.T. (1997) *Large Group Interventions: Engaging the Whole System for Rapid Change*. San Francisco, CA: Jossey-Bass.

Bureau of Air Safety Investigation (1996) *Human Factors in Fatal Aircraft Accident*, http://www.narcap.org/articles/HumanFactorsinFatalAircraftaccidents.pdf (accessed 25 January 2011).

Callow, S. (2010) Acting as narrative. In S. Corrie and D.A. Lane (eds) *Constructing Stories, Telling Tales: A Guide to Formulation in Applied Psychology*. London: Karnac, pp. 273–84.

Carkhuf, R.R. and Berenson, B.G. (1967) *Beyond Counselling and Therapy*. New York: Holt, Rinehart and Winston.

Carroll, M. (1996) *Counselling Supervision: Theories, Skills and Practice*. London: Cassell.

Castonguay, L.G., Goldfried, M.R., Wiser, S., Raue, P.J. and Hayes, A.M. (1996) Predicting the effect of cognitive therapy for depression: a study of unique and common factors. *Journal of Consulting and Clinical Psychology*, 64: 497–504.

Cavanagh, M. and Lane, D.A. (2012) Coaching psychology coming of age: the challenges we face in the messy world of complexity? *International Coaching Psychology Review*, 7: 75–90.

Chan, D. (2010) Why patients are saying 'I want to be bipolar'. BBC News, 16 June. http://news.bbc.co.uk/1/hi/health/8609461.stm (accessed 24 August 2011).

Chapman, L. (2010) *Integrated Experiential Coaching: Becoming an Executive Coach*. London: Karnac.

Chen, G., Donahue, L.M. and Klimoski, R.J. (2004) Training undergraduates to work in organizational teams. *Academy of Management Learning and Education*, 3(1): 27–40.

Chen, M., Froehle, T. and Morran, K. (1997) Deconstructing dispositional bias in clinical inference: two interventions. *Journal of Counseling and Development*, 76: 74–81.

Clarkson, P. (2000) Eclectic, integrative and integrating psychotherapy or beyond schoolism. In S. Palmer, and R. Woolfe (eds) *Integrative and Eclectic Counselling and Psychotherapy*. London: Sage, pp. 305–14.

Cohen, M.B. (1998) Perceptions of power in client/worker relationships. *Families in Society: The Journal of Contemporary Human Services*, 79: 433–42.

Cohen, S.G. and Ledford, G.E. (1994) The effectiveness of self-managing teams: a quasi-experiment. *Human Relations*, 47: 13–43.

Corrie, S. (2009) *The Art of Inspired Living*. London: Karnac.

Corrie, S. (2010) What is evidence? In R. Woolfe, S. Strawbridge, B. Douglas and W. Dryden (eds) *Handbook of Counselling Psychology*, 3rd edn. London: Sage, pp. 44–61.

Corrie, S. and Lane, D.A. (2010) *Constructing Stories, Telling Tales: A Guide to Formulation in Applied Psychology*. London: Karnac.

Cotton, K. (1991) *Teaching Thinking Skills*, http://www.nwrel.org/sepd/sirs/6/cu11/html (accessed 22 June 2010).

Crabtree, M. (1998) Images of reasoning: a literature review. *Australian Occupational Therapy Journal*, 45: 113–23.

Curtis, K.A. (1994) Attributional analysis of interpersonal role conflict. *Social Science and Medicine*, 39(2): 255–63.

Dallos, R. and Draper, R. (2005) *Introduction to Family Therapy: Systemic Theory and Practice*, 2nd edn. Maidenhead: Open University Press.

Davison, G.C. (1991) Constructionism and therapy for homosexuality. *Clinical Psychology: Science and Practice*, 1: 157–68.

Davison, G.C. and Gann, M.K. (1998) The reformulation of panic attacks and a successful cognitive-behavioural treatment of social evaluative anxiety. In M. Bruch, and F.W. Bond (eds), *Beyond Diagnosis: Case Formulation Approaches in CBT*. Chichester: Wiley, pp. 65–80.

de Bono, E. (1985) *Six Thinking Hats: An Essential Approach to Business Management*. Boston, MA: Little, Brown & Co.

de Bono, E. (1995) *Parallel Thinking*. London: Penguin.

de Bono, E. (2006) The scientist–practitioner as thinker: a comment on judgment and design. In D.A. Lane, and S. Corrie (eds), *The Modern Scientist–Practitioner: A Guide to Practice in Psychology*. Hove: Routledge, pp. 173–85.

Department of Health (2003) *Clinical Supervision in the Workplace: Guidance for Occupational Health Nurses*. London: Department of Health.

Department of Health (2004) *Organising and Delivering Psychological Therapies*. London: Department of Health.

Department of Health (2008) *IAPT: Improving Access to Psychological Therapies*, http://www.iapt.nhs.uk (accessed 20 July 2011).

Deslauriers, D. (1992) Dimensions of knowing: narrative, paradigm, and ritual, *ReVision*, 14(4): 187–93.

Dowie, J.A. and Elstein, A.S. (1988) *Professional Judgement: A Reader in Clinical Decision Making*. Cambridge: Cambridge University Press.

Edmondson, A. (1999) Psychological safety and learning behaviour in work teams, *Administrative Science Quarterly*, 44: 350–83.

Edmondson, A.C. (2002) The local and variegated nature of learning in organizations: A group-level perspective, *Organization Science*, 13(2): 128–46.

Edwards, L. (2002) Clinical psychologists' decision-making processes during therapy assessment: a qualitative study. Unpublished D.Clin.Psychol. thesis, Canterbury Christchurch University College.

Emerson, S. (1996) Creating a safe place for growth in supervision. *Contemporary Family Therapy*, 18: 393–403.

Ericsson, K.A. and Smith, J. (1991) *Toward a General Theory of Expertise*. Cambridge: Cambridge University Press.

Farrell, B.A. (1979) Work in small groups: some philosophical considerations. In B. Babbington Smith and B.A. Farrell (eds), *Training in Small Groups: A Study of Five Methods*. Oxford: Pergammon, pp. 103–115.

Försterling, F. (1988) *Attribution Theory in Clinical Psychology* (trans. by Jonathan Harrow). Chichester: Wiley.

Friedlander, M.L. and Ward, L.G. (1984) Development and validation of the Sueprvisory Styles Inventory, *Journal of Counseling Psychology*, 31(4): 541–57.

Gambrill, E. (2005) *Critical Thinking in Clinical Practice*, 2nd edn. Hoboken, NJ: Wiley.

Gendlin, E. (1996) *Focusing-oriented Psychotherapy: A Manual of the Experiential Method*. New York: Guilford Press.

Gendlin, E. (1997) *Experiencing and the Creation of Meaning*. Evanston, IL: Northwestern University Press. Also http://www.focusing.org/gendlin/gol_primary_bibliography.htm and http://www.focusing.org/gendlin/ and www.youtube.com/watch?v=j7PEC5Mh5FY (accessed 12 August 2011).

Gosling, P. (2010) Every child does matter: preventing school exclusion through the Common Assessment Framework. In S. Corrie and D.A. Lane (eds), *Constructing Stories, Telling Tales: A Guide to Formulation in Applied Psychology*. London: Karnac, pp. 173–98.

Greenfield, L.B. (1987) Teaching thinking through problem solving. In J.E. Stice (ed.), *Developing Critical Thinking and Problem-solving Abilities*. San Francisco, CA: Jossey-Bass, pp. 5–36.

Guest, P.D. and Beutler, L.E. (1988) Impact of psychotherapy supervision on therapist orientation and values. *Journal of Consulting and Clinical Psychology*, 56: 653–58.

Guzzo, R.A. and Shea, G.P. (1992) Group performance and intergroup relations in organizations. In M.D. Dunnette and L.M. Hough (eds), *Handbook of Industrial and Organizational Psychology*, Volume 3. Palo Alto, CA: Consulting Psychologists Press, pp. 269–313.

Hackman, J.R. (2002) *Leading Teams: Setting the Stage for Great Performances.* Boston, MA: Harvard Business School Press.

Hardman, D. (2009) *Judgment and Decision Making: Psychological Perspectives.* Oxford: BPS Blackwell.

Harvey, J.B. (1996) *The Abilene Paradox and Other Meditations on Management.* San Francisco, CA: Jossey-Bass.

Hawkins, P. (2011) *Leadership Team Coaching: Developing Collective Transformational Leadership.* London: Kogan Page.

Heider, F. (1958) *The Psychology of Interpersonal Relations.* New York: Wiley.

Her Majesty's Inspectorate (1978) *Behavioural Units.* London: Department of Education and Science.

Hess, A.K. (1980) *Psychotherapy Supervision: Theory, Research and Practice.* New York: Wiley.

Hillman, J. (1983) *Healing Fiction.* Dallas, TX: Spring.

Hogarth, R. (1981) Beyond discrete biases: functional and dysfunctional aspects of judgmental heuristics. *Psychological Bulletin*, 90: 197–217.

Holloway, E.L. (1997) Structures for the analysis and teaching of supervision. In C.E. Watkins (ed.), *Handbook of Psychotherapy Supervision.* New York: Wiley, pp. 249–76.

Intrator, J., Allan, E. and Palmer, M. (1992) Decision tree for the management of substance-abusing psychiatric patients, *Journal of Substance Abuse Treatment*, 9: 215–20.

Ivey, D.C., Scheel, M.J. and Jankowski, P.J. (1999) A contextual perspective of clinical judgement in couples and family therapy: is the bridge too far? *Journal of Family Therapy*, 21(4): 339–59.

Isenberg, D.J. (1986) Group polarization: a critical review, *Journal of Personality and Social Psychology*, 50: 1141–51.

Janis, I.L. (1972) *Victims of Groupthink.* Boston, MA: Houghton Mifflin.

Jordan, L. (2010) Relational trauma. In R. Woolfe, S. Strawbridge, B. Douglas and W. Dryden (eds), *Handbook of Counselling Psychology.* London: Sage, pp. 235–256.

Josselson, R. and Lieblich, A. (2003) *Making Meaning of Narratives, Volume 6.* Thousand Oaks, CA: Sage.

Kahane, A. (2007) *Solving Tough Problems: An Open Way of Listening and Creating New Realities.* San Francisco, CA: Berrett-Koehler.

Kahneman, D., Slovic, P. and Tversky, A. (1982) *Judgement under Uncertainty: Heuristics and Biases*. New York: Cambridge University Press.

Kaiser, T.L. (1992) The supervisory relationship: an identification of the primary elements in the relationship and an application of two theories of ethical relationships. *Journal of Marital and Family Therapy*, 18: 283–96.

Kassirer, J.P., Kuipers, B.J. and Gorry, G.A. (1982) Towards a theory of clinical expertise, *American Journal of Medicine*, 73(2): 251–9.

Kayes, D.C. (2006) *Destructive Goal Pursuit: The Mount Everest Disaster*. Basingstoke: Palgrave.

Kelley, H.H. (1967) Attribution theory in social psychology. In D. Levine (ed.), *Nebraska Symposium on Motivation*. Lincoln, NE: University of Nebraska Press.

Kline, N. (2003) *Time to Think: Listening to Ignite the Human Mind*. London: Ward Lock.

Kline, N. (2005) *The Thinking Partnership Programme: Consultants Guide*. Wallingford: Time to Think.

Kolb, D.A. (1984) *Experiential Learning: Experience as the Source of Learning and Development*. Englewood Cliffs, NJ: Prentice Hall.

Koriat, A., Lichtenstein, S. and Fischhoff, B. (1980) Reasons for confidence, *Journal of Experimental Psychology: Human Learning and Memory*, 6: 107–18.

Kozlowski, S.W.J. and Ilgen, D.R. (2006) Enhancing the effectiveness or work groups and teams, *Psychological Science in the Public Interest*, 7(3), 77–124.

Krakauer, J. (1998) *Into Thin Air: A Personal Account of the Everest Disaster*. London: Pan.

Krogerus, M. and Tschäppeler, R. (2008) *The Decision Book: Fifty Models for Strategic Thinking*. Zurich: Kein und Auber.

Kwiatkowski, R. and Winter, B. (2006) Roots, relativity and realism: the occupational psychologist as scientist-practitioner. In D.A. Lane and S. Corrie (eds), *The Modern Scientist–Practitioner: A Guide to Practice in Psychology*. Hove: Routledge, pp. 158–172.

Ladany, N. (2004) Psychotherapy supervision: what lies beneath, *Psychotherapy Research*, 14: 1–19.

Lambert, M.J. (1980) Research and the supervisory process, in A.K. Hess (ed.), *Psychotherapy Supervision: Theory, Research and Practice*. New York: Wiley, pp. 423–50.

Lane, D.A. (1973) Pathology of communication: a pitfall in community health, *Community Health*, 5(3): 157–62.

Lane, D.A. (1996) What works, *Forensic Update*, 44: 30–2.

Lane, D.A. (2011) Ethics and professional standards in supervision, in T. Bachkirova, P. Jackson and D. Clutterbuck (eds), *Coaching and Mentoring Supervision*. Maidenhead: Open University Press.

Lane, D.A. and Corrie, S. (2006) *The Modern Scientist–Practitioner: A Guide to Practice in Psychology*. Hove: Routledge.

Lane, D., Pumain, D., van der Leeuw S. and West G. (2009) *Complexity Perspectives on Innovation and Social Change*. Berlin: Springer-Verlag.

Lazare, A. (1976) The psychiatric examination in the walk-in clinic, *Archives of General Psychiatry*, 33: 96–102.

Leahy, R (2003) *Roadblocks in Cognitive-Behavioral Therapy*. New York: Guilford Press.

Leary, M.R. (1999) Making sense of self-esteem, *Current Directions in Psychological Science*, 8(1): 32–5.

Lewis, R. (1986) *Method or Madness?* London: Methuen.

Liese, B.S. and Beck, J.S (1997) Cognitive therapy supervision. In C.E. Watkins (ed.), *Handbook of Psychotherapy Supervision*. New York: Wiley, pp. 114–33.

Light, R.J. (2001) *Making the Most of College: Students Speak Their Minds*. Cambridge: MA: Harvard University Press.

Livingston, S. (1997) *The Work of Elihu Katz: Conceptualizing Media Effects in Context*. http://eprints.lse.ac.uk/998/ (accessed 12 August 2011).

Locke, E.A. and Latham, G.P. (1990) *A Theory of Goal Setting and Task Performance*. Englewood Cliffs, NJ: Prentice Hall.

Lord, C., Lepper, M., and Ross, L. (1979) Biased assimilation and attitude polarization: the effects of prior theories on subsequently considered evidence, *Journal of Personality and Social Psychology*, 37: 2098–110.

Luborsky, L. and Crits-Cristoph, P. (1990) *Understanding Transference: The Core Conflictual Relationship Themes Method*. New York: Basic Books.

Lucock, M.P., Hall, P. and Noble, R. (2006) A survey of influences on the practice of psychotherapists and clinical psychologists in training in the UK, *Clinical Psychology and Psychotherapy*, 13: 123–30.

McCann, D. (2011) Supervision: making it work for you. In R. Bor and M. Watts (eds), *The Trainee Handbook: A Guide for Counselling and Psychotherapy Trainees*, 3rd edn. London: Sage, pp. 203–222.

McLeod, J. (2000) Guest editorial: the development of narrative-informed theory, research and practice in counselling and psychotherapy: European perspectives, *European Journal of Psychotherapy, Counselling & Health*, 3(3): 331–3.

McNeill, B.W., Stoltenberg, C.D. and Romans, J.S.C. (1992) The integrated developmental model of supervision: scale development and validation procedures, *Professional Psychology: Research and Practice*, 23: 504–8.

Mahrer, A.R. (2000) Philosophy of science and the foundations of psychotherapy, *American Psychologist*, 55(10): 1117–25.

Martell, C.R., Addis, M.E. and Jacobson, N.S. (2001) *Depression in Context: Strategies for Guided Action*. New York: Norton.

Meehl, P.E (1954) *Clinical versus Statistical Prediction: A Theoretical Analysis and a Review of the Evidence*. Minneapolis, MN: University of Minnesota Press.

Meehl, P.E (1957) When shall we use our heads instead of the formula? *Journal of Counselling Psychology*, 4: 268–73.

Meehl, P.E (1997) Credentialed persons, credentialed knowledge, *Clinical Psychology: Science and Practice*, 4(2): 91–8.

Merlin, B. (2003) *Konstantin Stanislavsky*. Abingdon: Routledge.

Merton, R.K. (1938) Social structure and anomie, *American Sociological Review*, 3(5): 672–82.

Milne, D. (2009) *Evidence-based Clinical Supervision: Principles and Practice*. Oxford: BPS Blackwell.

Milne, D.L., Leck, C. and Choudhri, N. (2009) Collusion in clinical practice: literature review and case study in self-reflection, *The Cognitive Behaviour Therapist*, 2: 106–14.

Moscovici, S. and Zavalloni, M. (1969) The group as a polarizer of attitudes, *Journal of Personality and Social Psychology*, 12: 125–35.

Murphy, M.J. and Wright, D.W. (2005) Supervisees' perspectives of power use in supervision, *Journal of Marital and Family Therapy*, 31(3): 283–95.

Myers, D.G. (2005) *Social Psychology*, 8th edn. New York: McGraw Hill.

Nelson, M. L. and Friedlander, M. L. (2001) A close look at conflictual supervisory relationships: the trainee's perspective, *Journal of Counseling Psychology*, 48: 384–95.

O'Donohue, W., Fisher, J.E., Plaud, J.J. and Curtis, S.D. (1990) Treatment decisions: their nature and their justification, *Psychotherapy*, 27(3): 421–7.

O'Donohue, W. and Henderson, D. (1999) Epistemic and ethical duties in clinical decision-making, *Behaviour Change*, 16(1): 10–19.

O'Neill, M.B. (2007) *Executive Coaching with Backbone and Heart: A Systems Approach to Engaging Leaders with Their Challenges*, 2nd edn. San Francisco, CA: Jossey-Bass.

Oskamp, S. (1965) Overconfidence in case-study judgments, *Journal of Consulting Psychology*, 29: 261–5.

Owen, J., and Lindley, L.D. (2010) Therapists' cognitive complexity: review of theoretical models and development of an integrated approach for training, *Training and Education in Professional Psychology*, 4(2): 128–37.

Pascale, R.T. Millemann, M. and Gioja, L. (2000) *Surfing the Edge of Chaos: The Laws of Nature and the New Laws of Business*. New York: Crown Books.

Paul, R.W. (1993) *Critical Thinking: What Every Person Needs to Survive in a Rapidly Changing World*. Santa Rosa, CA: Foundation for Critical Thinking.

Paul, R.W. and Elder, L. (2002) *Critical Thinking: Tools for Taking Charge of your Professional and Personal Life*. Upper Saddle River, NJ: Financial Times/Prentice Hall.

Polkinghorne, D.E. (1992) Postmoderm epistemology of practice. In S. Kvale (ed.), *Psychology and Postmodernism*. London: Sage, pp. 146–65.

Porter, N., and Vasquez, M. (1997) Covision: feminist supervision, process, and collaboration. In J. Worell and N. G. Johnson (eds), *Shaping the Future of Feminist Psychology*. Washington, DC: American Psychological Association, pp. 155–71.

Proctor, B. (1986) Supervision: a cooperative exercise in accountability. In A. Marken and M. Payne (eds), *Enabling and Ensuring: Supervision in Practice*. Leicester: National Youth Bureau/Council for Education and Training in Youth and Community Work.

Rajan, A., van Eupen, P., Chapple, K. and Lane D.A. (2000) *Employability. Bridging the Gap between Rhetoric and Reality. First Report: Employers' Perspective*. Tonbridge: Create/PDF/CIPD.

Ramos-Sánchez, L., Esnil, E., Goodwin, A., Riggs, S., Touster, L.O., Wright, L.K., Ratanasiripong, P. and Rodolfa, E. (2002) Negative supervisory events: effects on supervision and supervisory alliance, *Professional Psychology: Research and Practice*, 33(2): 197–202.

Righetti, P.L., Avanzo, M.D., Grigio, M. and Nicolini, U. (2005) Maternal/paternal antenatal attachment and fourth-dimensional ultrasound technique: a preliminary report, *British Journal of Psychology*, 96: 1–10.

Roth, A.D. and Pilling, S. (2007) *The Competences Required to Deliver Effective Cognitive and Behavioural Therapy for Depression and Anxiety Disorders*. IAPT Programme, Department of Health. http://www.ucl.ac.uk/clinical-psychology/CORE/CBT_Framework.htm (accessed 24 August 2011).

Round, A.P. (1999) Teaching clinical reasoning: a preliminary controlled study, *Medical Education*, 33: 480–83.

Scales, P. and West, T. (2010) Understanding character: an actor's approach to formulation. In S. Corrie and D.A. Lane (eds), *Constructing Stories, Telling Tales: A Guide to Formulation in Applied Psychology*. London: Karnac, pp. 285–318.

Scaturo, D.J. and McPeak, W.R. (1998) Clinical dilemmas I. Contemporary psychotherapy: the search for clinical wisdom, *Psychotherapy*, 35(1): 1–12.

Senge, P., Scharmer, O., Jaworski, J. and Flowers, B.S. (2005) *Presence Exploring Profound Change in People, Organizations and Society*. London: Nicolas Brealey.

Seidenstücker, G. and Roth, W.L. (1998) Treatment decisions: types, models and schools, *European Journal of Psychological Assessment*, 14(1): 2–13.

Shafran, R., Clark, D.M., Fairburn, C.G., Arntz, A., Barlow, D.H., Ehlers, A., Freeston, M., Garety, P.A., Hollon, S.D., Ost, L.G., Salkovskis, P.M., Williams, J.M.G. and Wilson, G.T. (2009) Mind the gap: improving the dissemination of CBT. *Behaviour Research and Therapy*, 47: 902–9.

Shweder, R.A. (1977) Likeness and likelihood in everyday thought: magical thinking in judgments about personality, *Current Anthropology*, 18: 637–48.

Siegert, R.J. (1999) Some thoughts about reasoning in clinical neuropsychology, *Behaviour Change*, 16(1): 37–48.

Snowdon, D.J. and Boone, M.E. (2007) A leader's framework for decision making, *Harvard Business Review*, November, 61–8.

Sobell, M.B. and Sobell, L.C. (2000) Stepped care as a heuristic approach to the treatment of alcohol problems, *Journal of Consulting and Clinical Psychology*, 68(4): 573–9.

Stacey, R.D. (2002) *Strategic Management and Organisational Dynamics: The Challenge of Complexity*, 3rd edn. Harlow: Prentice Hall.

Sterman, J.D. (1994) Learning in and about complex systems, *System Dynamics Review*, 10(2/3): 291–330.

Stevens, M.J. and Campion, M.A. (1994) The knowledge, skills and ability requirements for teamwork: implications for human resources management, *Journal of Management*, 20(2): 502–28.

Stice, J.E. (1987) *Developing Critical Thinking and Problem-solving Abilities*. San Francisco, CA: Jossey-Bass.

Stoltenberg, C. (1981) Approaching supervision from a developmental perspective: the counsellor complexity model, *Journal of Counseling Psychology*, 28(1): 59–65.

Stoltenberg, C.D. and Delworth, V. (1987) *Developmental Supervision: A Training Model for Counsellors and Psychotherapists*. San Francisco, CA: Jossey-Bass.

Stoltenberg, C. McNeill, B.W. and Crethar, H.C. (1994) Changes in supervision as counselors and therapists gain experience: a review, *Professional Psychology: Research and Practice*, 25(4): 416–49.

Stoner, J.A.F. (1961) A comparison of individual and group decisions including risk. Unpublished master's thesis, Massachusetts Institute of Technology, Boston.

Strasser, F. and Strasser, A. (1997) *Existential Time-limited Therapy: The Wheel of Existence*. Chichester: Wiley.

Tatar, M. (2003). *Classic Fairy Tales*. New York: Norton.

Taylor, A.J.W. and Lane, D.A. (eds) (1991) Psychological aspects of disaster: issues for the 1990s, *British Journal of Guidance and Counselling*, Special Issue, 19(1).

Teasdale, J.D. and Barnard, P.J. (1993) *Affect, Cognition and Change: Remodelling Depressive Thought*. Hove: Erlbaum.

Turk, D.C. and Salovey, P. (1985) Cognitive structures, cognitive processes, and cognitive-behaviour modification: II. Judgments and inferences of the clinician, *Cognitive Therapy and Research*, 9(1): 19–33.

Turpin, G. (2001) Single case methodology and psychotherapy evaluation: from research to practice. In C. Mace, S. Moorey and B. Roberts (eds), *Evidence in the Psychological Therapies: A Critical Guide for Practitioners*. Hove: Brunner-Routledge, pp. 91–113.

Tversky, A. and Kahneman, D. (1973) Availability: a heuristic for judging frequency and probability, *Cognitive Psychology*, 5: 207–32.

Tversky, A. and Kahneman, D. (1974) Judgment under uncertainty: heuristics and biases, *Science*, 185: 1124–31.

Tversky, A. and Kahneman, D. (1980) Causal schemas in judgments under uncertainty. In M. Fishbein (ed.), *Progress in Social Psychology, Volume 1*. Hillsdale, NJ: Erlbaum, pp. 49–72.

Wampold, B.E. and Holloway, E.L. (1997) Methodology, design and evaluation in psychotherapy supervision research. In C.E. Watkins (ed.), *Handbook of Psychotherapy Supervision*. New York: Wiley, pp. 11–27.

Watkins, C.W. (1997) *Handbook of Psychotherapy Supervision*. New York: Wiley.

Weiner, B., Frieze, I.H., Kukla, A., Reed, L., Rest, S. and Rosenbaum, R.M. (1971) *Perceiving the Causes of Success and Failure*. New York: General Learning Press.

Westen, D., Novotny, C.M. and Thompson-Brenner, H. (2004) The empirical status of empirically supported psychotherapists: assumptions, findings and reporting in controlled clinical trials, *Psychological Bulletin*, 130: 631–63.

Wheatley, M. (1999) *Leadership and the New Science: Discovering Order in a Chaotic World*. San Francisco, CA: Berrett-Koehler.

White, M. and Epston, D. (1990) *Narrative Means to Therapeutic Ends*. New York: Norton.

Wilber, K. (2000) *Integral Psychology: Consciousness, Spirit, Psychology, Therapy*. Boston: Shambhala.

Williams, N. (1999) *The Work We Were Born to Do*. London: Element.

Witteman, C. and Koele, P. (1999) Explaining treatment decisions, *Psychotherapy Research*, 9(1): 100–14.

Witteman, C.L.M. and Kunst, H. (1999) Select care: in aid of psychotherapists' treatment decisions, *Computers in Human Behaviour*, 15(2): 143–59.

Young, J.E. (1994) *Cognitive Therapy for Personality Disorders: A Schema-Focused Approach*. Sarasota, FL: Professional Resource Press.

Author and Subject Index

abilene paradox, 155
accuracy (of decision making), 4, 6, 11, 12, 15–20, 22, 27, 29, 31, 32–35, 37, 39, 41, 43–44, 47, 73, 99, 101, 113–114, 166–167, 170–172
Adair, J., 108, 112, 114
ambiguity, 2, 14, 17, 42, 49–50, 52, 167
Anderson, H. and Swim, S., 140
Argyris, C., 159
Arkes, H.R., 18, 19
assumptive world (also assumptive worldview), 139–140
atttachment theory, 97
attitude (component of MAP), 4, 65–68, 78, 84, 87–90, 92, 100, 104–105, 107, 110, 139, 146
attribution theory, 20–21, 27, 90

Bandura, A. and Schunk, D.H., 168
Baxter Magolda, M.B., 88
Becher, E.C. and Chassin, M.R., 1
Beck, A.T., Rush, A.J., Shaw, B.F. and Emery, G., 23
Benedetti, J., 78
Bernard, J.M. and Goodyear, R.K., 136, 141, 165
Beyer, B.K., 40
biases (perceptual, interpretive), 11, 17–20, 22–25, 28–29, 31, 120, 127, 154, 155, 157, 171
Bieling, P.J. and Kuyken, W., 17
Blackburn, I.M., James, I.A., Milne, D.L., Baker, C., Standart, S., Garland, A. and Reichelt, K., 137
Bonosky, N., 138
Bowlby, J., 97
Brewin, C.R., 20
British Association for Counselling and Psychotherapy, 133, 134
British Psychological Society, 133, 134
Bruner, J.S., 40
Buber, M., 96

Buckland, D., 166
Bunker, B.B. and Alban, B.T., 161
Bureau of Air Safety Investigation, 154

Callow, S., 79
Carkhuf, R.R. and Berenson, B.G., 16
Carroll, M., 134
Castonguay, L.G., Goldfried, M.R., Wiser, S., Raue, P.J. and Hayes, A.M., 39
causal analysis, 18, 21–22
Cavanagh, M. and Lane, D.A., 51, 52, 59, 123
Chan, D., 90
chaotic space, 52–53, 61, 101
Chapman, L., 56, 161
Chen, G., Donahue, L.M. and Klimoski, R.J., 153
Chen, M., Froehle, T. and Morran, K., 20
Clarkson, P., 164
clinical judgement, 3, 4, 11, 16, 22, 31, 37
cognitive distortions, 23, 25, 28
Cohen, M.B., 138
Cohen, S.G. and Ledford, G.E., 159
complex perspective (*see also* complex space), 59, 61, 101
complex systems, 123
confirmatory bais, 22
conditions of uncertainty, 118
Corrie, S., 25, 28, 48, 66, 68
Corrie, S. and Lane, D.A., 34, 50, 51, 66, 83, 93, 101, 112, 124
Cost benefit analysis (also analysis of advantages and disadvantages), 114–116
Cotton, K., 7, 165
countertransference (*see also* transference), 99
Crabtree, M., 33
creativity, 121, 167
critical thinking, 109

culture of blame, 89
Curtis, K.A., 21

Dallos, R. and Draper, R., 101
Davison, G.C., 58
Davison, G.C. and Gann, M.K., 58
de Bono, E., 39, 44, 53
decision making biases, 88
decision-making tools, 1, 109, 112,
   118, 127
decision process, 120
decision quadrant, 72
deeper perspective, 57, 61
Department of Health 131, 133, 136
Depression, 89, 112
Design, 48
Deslauriers, D., 40
destructive goal pursuit (Kayes), 159,
   162
dialogue, 124
different perspective, 53
disaster management, 81
Dowie, J.A. and Elstein, A.S., 34, 37

Edmondson, A., 158
educational guidance centre, 82
Edwards, L., 37
emergent space, 52–53, 61, 101
Emerson, S., 138
Ericsson, K.A. and Smith, J., 2
exterior work (Stanislavski), 78–79

Farrell, B.A., 104
felt sense, 57–58, 125, 167, 172
fields of vision (*see also* personal
   perspective, interpersonal
   perspective and systemic
   perspective), 93, 95, 99, 103–104,
   111
fishing metaphor (de Bono) 39–40, 53
foundational assumptions, 32, 159, 173
Forsterling, F., 20
Friedlander, M.L. and Ward, L.G., 142

Gambrill, E., 15, 25
Gendlin, E., 57, 58, 166
gestalt, 154
goalodicy (Kayes), 159
Gosling, P., 112
Greenfield, L.B., 7
group polarization, 156

groupthink, 155
Guest, P.D. and Beutler, L.E., 144
Guzzo, R.A. and Shea, G.P., 152

Hackman, J.R., 153, 158
Hardman, D., 152, 155
Harvey, J.B., 155
Hawkins, P., 153, 161, 162
Heider, F., 20
Her Majesty's Inspectorate, 82
Heuristics (*see also* availability
   heuristic, representativeness,
   anchoring), 20–23, 27–28
Hess, A.K., 142, 144
Hillman, J., 41
Hogarth, R., 37
Holloway, E.L., 137

i thou (Buber), 96–97
ill-structured problems, 160
illusory correlation, 22
imaginal reliving (for PTSD), 114–116
implicational levels of meaning, 40–41,
   44, 47–48, 58, 172
information processing framework,
   33–34, 37
innovation, 3–4, 9, 39, 44, 47–48, 61,
   75, 113, 152, 167, 170
interior work (Stanislavski), 78
Intrator, J., Allan, E. and Palmer, M., 38
Ivey, D.C., Scheel, M.J. and Jankowski,
   P.J., 33
Isenberg, D.J., 156

Janis, I.L., 155
Jordan, L., 97
Josselson, R. and Lieblich, A., 121

Kahane, A., 123
Kahneman, D., Slovic, P. and Tversky,
   A., 21
Kaiser, T.L., 138
Kassirer, J.P., Kuipers, B.J. and Gorry,
   G.A., 2
Kayes, D.C., 152, 158, 159, 162
Kelley, H.H., 20
Kline, N., 55
Kolb, D.A., 56
Koriat, A., Lichtenstein, S. and
   Fischhoff, B., 19
Kozlowski, S.W.J. and Ilgen, D.R., 158

Krakauer, J., 154
Krogerus, M. and Tschappeler, R., 112
Kwiatkowski, R. and Winter, B., 29

Ladany, N., 138
Lambert, M.J., 144
Lane, D.A., 112, 133, 135
Lane, D.A. and Corrie, S., 34, 37, 38, 45, 65, 68, 93, 101, 133
Lane, D., Pumain, D., van der Leeuw S. and West G., 59
Lazare, A., 92, 93
Leahy, R., 14
Leary, M.R., 99
levels of influence (*see also* local, national and global levels of influence),100
Lewis, R., 78
Liese, B.S. and Beck, J.S., 133
Light, R.J., 153
Livingston, S., 59
Locke, E.A. and Latham, G.P., 39, 159
Lord, C., Lepper, M., and Ross, L., 22
Luborsky, L. and Crits-Cristoph, P., 17
Lucock, M.P., Hall, P. and Noble, R., 133

Mahrer, A.R., 32
manualized interventions, 38–39, 140
map (mission, attitude, process, introduction to), 65
Martell, C.R., Addis, M.E. and Jacobson, N.S., 89, 90
McCann, D., 138
McLeod, J., 41
McNeill, B.W., Stoltenberg, C.D. and Romans, J.S.C., 141
Meehl, P.E., 16, 17, 34
Merlin, B., 78
Merton, R.K., 59
messy system, 123
Milne, D., 134, 136, 140, 141, 148
Milne, D.L., Leck, C. and Choudhri, N., 135
mission (component of map), 4, 65–66, 68, 71–81, 83–84, 105, 107, 110, 135, 146
Mount Everest climbing disaster, 159
Moscovici, S. and Zavalloni, M., 156

Murphy, M.J. and Wright, D.W., 137, 138
Myers, D.G., 156

narrative knowledge (*see also* implicational levels of meaning), 40, 44, 47
narrative content, 125
narrative process, 124
narrative structure, 124
Nelson, M. L. and Friedlander, M. L., 138

O'Donohue, W., Fisher, J.E., Plaud, J.J. and Curtis, S.D., 3
O'Donohue, W. and Henderson, D., 16, 17, 18, 22
O'Neill, M.B., 100, 102, 104
Oskamp, S., 16
Owen, J., and Lindley, L.D., 42, 165

paradigmatic knowledge (*see also* propositional levels of meaning), 40–41, 52, 125
Pascale, R.T. Millemann, M. and Gioja, L., 51
Paul, R.W., 168
Paul, R.W. and Elder, L., 91, 154
perspectives on change (*see also* fields of vision), 93–96, 99
Polkinghorne, D.E., 104
Porter, N., and Vasquez, M., 138
Proctor, B., 136
professional spaces, 53, 135, 168
propositional levels of meaning (*see also* paradigmatic knowledge), 40, 44, 52, 57, 125, 172
protocols, 38

quadrant, 69, 72–76, 80, 84, 88, 95, 101, 110–112, 116, 118, 123–124, 127, 168–169

Rajan, A., van Eupen, P., Chapple, K. and Lane D.A., 50
Ramos-Sanchez, L., Esnil, E., Goodwin, A., Riggs, S., Touster, L.O., Wright, L.K., Ratanasiripong, P. and Rodolfa, E., 133
rational space, 51, 61, 101
reasoning styles, 2, 4

reflective tool, 4, 170
Righetti, P.L., Avanzo, M.D., Grigio, M.
 and Nicolini, U., 97
risky shift, 156
Roth, A.D. and Pilling, S., 134
Round, A.P., 20

Scales, P. and West, T., 78
Scaturo, D.J. and McPeak, W.R., 14, 37
schema, 23–24
secure base (*see also* attachment
 theory), 97
self-esteem, 97
Senge, P., Scharmer, O., Jaworski, J.
 and Flowers, B.S., 57, 58, 59
Seidenstucker, G. and Roth, W.L., 38
Shafran, R., Clark, D.M., Fairburn,
 C.G., Arntz, A., Barlow, D.H.,
 Ehlers, A., Freeston, M., Garety,
 P.A., Hollon, S.D., Ost, L.G.,
 Salkovskis, P.M., Williams, J.M.G.
 and Wilson, G.T., 17
shooting metaphor (de Bono), 39, 40,
 53
Shweder, R.A., 23
Siegert, R.J., 34
Snowdon, D.J. and Boone, M.E., 52
Sobell, M.B. and Sobell, L.C., 35
social interactional field, 100
social loafing, 155
Stacey, R.D., 51
stepped approach to decision-making,
 113–114, 121, 123
Sterman, J.D., 17
Stevens, M.J. and Campion, M.A., 153
Stice, J.E., 1, 42
Stoltenberg, C., 141
Stoltenberg, C.D. and Delworth, V.,
 141, 144, 145
Stoltenberg, C. McNeill, B.W. and
 Crethar, H.C., 143, 144
Stoner, J.A.F., 156
Strasser, F. and Strasser, A., 50

super objective (Stanislavski), 78–79,
 81, 83
supervision, 4, 6, 12, 29, 131–134, 148,
 171
 as apprenticeship, 135–136
 functions of: normative, formative,
  restorative, 137
 integrated development model, 141,
  144
 models of, 141
 power, issues of, 137–138

Tatar, M., 41
Taylor, A.J.W. and Lane, D.A., 82
Teasdale, J.D. and Barnard, P.J., 40
Teams,
 Decision-making in, 151–152
 high performing, 161
 learning in, 153, 161
through line of action (Stanislavski), 79
transference, 99
Turk, D.C. and Salovey, P., 82
Turpin, G., 17
Tversky, A. and Kahneman, D., 21, 22

uncertainty, 6, 15, 47, 59, 61

Wampold, B.E. and Holloway, E.L., 133
Watkins, C.W., 139, 143
Weiner, B., Frieze, I.H., Kukla, A., Reed,
 L., Rest, S. and Rosenbaum, R.M.,
 20
Westen, D., Novotny, C.M. and
 Thompson-Brenner, H., 39
Wheatley, M., 108
White, M. and Epston, D., 101
Wider perspective, 53, 55, 61
Wilber, K., 56
Williams, N., 170
Witteman, C. and Koele, P., 23, 24
Witteman, C.L.M. and Kunst, H., 38

Young, J.E., 23, 24

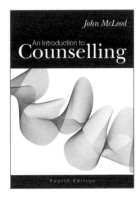

An Introduction to Counselling
Fourth Edition

John McLeod

9780335225514 (Paperback)
2009

eBook also available

This thoroughly revised and expanded version of the bestselling text, *An Introduction to Counselling*, provides a comprehensive introduction to the theory and practice of counselling and therapy. It is written in a clear, accessible style, covers all the core approaches to counselling, and takes a critical, questioning approach to issues of professional practise.

Placing each counselling approach in its social and historical context, the book also introduces a wide range of contemporary approaches, including transactional analysis, arts-based approaches and the use of natural environment in counselling.

Key features:

- Includes commonly used key terms and concepts
- Includes case studies and illustrations relevant to everyday practice
- Chapters covering the integrating of theory into practice

www.openup.co.uk

The Handbook of Transcultural Counselling and Psychotherapy
First Edition

Colin Lago

9780335238491 (Paperback)
Nov 2011

eBook also available

This fascinating book examines recent critical thinking and contemporary research findings in the field of transcultural counselling and psychotherapy. It also explores the effects of different cultural heritages upon potential clients and therapists.

Key features:

- Covers key issues such as: the implications of identity development for therapeutic work; ethnic matching of clients and therapists and working with interpreters and bi-cultural workers.
- Examines ways to overcome racism, discrimination and oppression within the counselling process.
- Provides an overview of current research within this field.

www.openup.co.uk

OPEN UNIVERSITY PRESS
McGraw - Hill Education